INDIGENOUS HISTORICAL KNOWLEDGE

Kautilya and His Vocabulary

VOLUME I

INDIGENOUS HISTORICAL KNOWLEDGE

Kautilya and His Vocabulary

VOLUME I

Editors

Pradeep Kumar Gautam

Saurabh Mishra

Arvind Gupta

INSTITUTE FOR DEFENCE STUDIES & ANALYSES
NEW DELHI

PENTAGON PRESS

Indigenous Historical Knowledge: Kautilya and His Vocabulary

Pradeep Kumar Gautam, Saurabh Mishra and Arvind Gupta (Editors)

First Published in 2015

ISBN 978-81-8274-849-1

Disclaimer: The views expressed in this book are those of the authors and do not necessarily reflect those of the Institute for Defence Studies and Analyses, or the Government of India.

Published by

PENTAGON PRESS
206, Peacock Lane, Shahpur Jat,
New Delhi-110049
Phones: 011-64706243, 26491568
Telefax: 011-26490600
email: rajan@pentagonpress.in
website: www.pentagonpress.in

Branch

Flat No.213, Athena-2,
Clover Acropolis,
Viman Nagar,
Pune-411014
Email: pentagonpresspune@gmail.com

In association with

Institute for Defence Studies and Analyses
No. 1, Development Enclave,
New Delhi-110010
Phone: +91-11-26717983
Website: www.idsa.in

Printed at Aegean Offset Printers, Greater Noida, U.P.

Contents

Preface

This book consists of various deliberations on the different aspects of the Kautilyan *Arthashastra*, its relevance and importance. It is a product of two workshops organised by the Institute for Defence Studies and Analyses (IDSA). The first "Workshop on Kautilya" was organised on October 18, 2012 that focused on revitalising Kautilya and his ideas in the strategic and diplomatic domains. The workshop was organised to disseminate the idea that Kautilya needs to be relooked in the contemporary context and re-read to find out its explanatory value for the strategic and foreign policy problems that the world in general and India in particular are facing these days. The exercise began with a belief that India did have systematic strategic thinking which was marginalised due to certain historical and social reasons. It was in a sense to overcome the burden of allegations that India does not have a strategic thinking. The larger goal was to sensitise the strategic community with the Kautilyan ideas, which were hitherto largely in the domain of Sanskritists, and their relevance so that they could have confidence in parts of their indigenous selves and thinking. The second workshop titled "Workshop on Kautilya: Creating Strategic Vocabulary" was organised on April 9, 2013 that specifically focused on the possible use of the Kautilyan vocabulary for the description and explanation of contemporary international scenario and problems. The participants were from the academic, military and diplomatic domains.

However, the discussions during the workshops resonated that though it is necessary to identify and study our indigenous knowledge, the specific call for an Indian strategic or international relations theory is absurd. But there is a definite need to regain the Indian past and confidence by setting it free from allegations of strategic dumbness. "The study of the text like *Arthashastra* is important not because they would provide us with the vocabulary and perspective for initiating an Indian theory of International Relations (IR), but because it would enable the Indian scholars to introduce nuances that may be missing in the Western discourse on IR and thus provide the scope for integrating Indian IR scholarship with the international mainstream." It was a common agreement among the scholars that "India urgently needs an Indian discourse of International Relations than Indian International Relations Theory." The two workshops were two initial steps by the IDSA in setting up this discourse. The institute has undertaken a reading of Kautilya to explore into the underexplored realm of the Indian indigenous historical knowledge. We hope this volume would add to the understanding of Kautilya and contribute to stir a debate on his theoretical credentials.

For transliteration of the Sanskrit words into English, we have not used the diacritical marks; for example, in the word *Arthaśāstra*. So, we have written 'the *Arthashastra*' instead of 'the *Arthaśāstra*.' However, in some places, the authors have used diacritical marks while referring to texts. Several authors and translators have not used diacritical marks, therefore we have kept them as they are.

August 2015 **Editors**

Opening Remarks by Dr Arvind Gupta, DG, IDSA at Workshop on Kautilya

October 18, 2012

National Security Adviser,
Participants of the workshop,
Friends,

It gives me great pleasure to welcome you to the Institute for Defence Studies and Analyses (IDSA) Workshop on Kautilya. I am particularly grateful to Shri Shivshankar Menon, the National Security Adviser, for readily agreeing to our request to inaugurate today's event. Shri Menon has been a supporter of IDSA's efforts to promote strategic thinking. His presence here today will give a boost to IDSA's Project on Indigenous Historical Knowledge. The Workshop on Kautilya is the opening event.

The workshop has been the brain-child of Col. P.K. Gautam (Retd.). Col. Gautam has been passionate about establishing the relevance of Kautilya's *Arthshastra* in contemporary security studies. In a recent paper, Col. Gautam has pointed out how Kautilya has not been treated fairly in the academic fields of political science, *realpolitik*, geopolitics and statecraft. He has also made a case for scholars and policymakers to re-visit Kautilya and study his work from different dimensions. Col. Gautam has worked hard for several months to organise this event.

We hope to achieve three key goals from the workshop today. First, we would like to bring together Indian scholars and experts, who have been studying Kautilya and have more than passing interest in his work. The group of scholars, who have gathered today, will hopefully be expanded further.

Second, we would like to establish that India has a long tradition of strategic thinking, which needs to be brought to light. Western scholars have held and many Indians agree that India has no culture of strategic thought. Nothing can be farther from the truth. We need to rediscover India's strategic thought. We do not know enough about it. In the recent years, Chinese strategic thinkers like Sun Tzu have become a rage with international scholars. Machiavelli, well-known to many, is perhaps a minor figure when compared to Chanakya (Kautilya). Indian scholars of IR, Political Science, Security Studies, Foreign policy should consciously base their research on Indian strategic thought and practices. Kautilya should get his well-deserved place in security studies within and outside the country. We hope that studies pertaining to indigenous historical thought will become more popular in the universities and think-tanks and younger scholars will be attracted to them.

Third, it is our hope that through the studies of Kautilya, impetus will be given to the study of regional literature, thinking of other Indian thinkers and strategists, who wrote and spoke in regional languages. We also need to rediscover the *Panchtantra*, the *Mahabharata* and Tamil *Sangam* literature to better appreciate Indian strategic thought.

Although it is believed that Kautilya's works were discovered in 1905, there are a few books in the British library which were published in the nineteenth century. For instance, there is reference in the catalogue to a book published by Capt. N. Chiefale on Kautilya published in Rome in 1825. In 1867, a book titled *Laghuchanikoraja Nitishastra* was published in 1867 in Gujarat. In 1887, a book titled *Chanakya* was published in Paris by E. Maneoseur. In 1891, Ramachandra Ghosh published a book on morals of Chanakya in Calcutta. These books are available in the British library. A serious effort should be made to collect and study these and other works and to explore whether there was an interest in Chanakya and his *Arthashastra* even in earlier times.

India abounded in regional Chanakyas too. A number of European travelers, who came to India in 15th-16th century and visited different parts of India, have written about the kingdoms and rivalries among them. Some of these writings indicate the prevalence of practical thinking in different kingdoms.

Today's workshop is a modest first effort towards encouraging a systematic thinking on India's strategic thought.

I must add here that this effort will remain a onetime affair unless it is supported by the government. We have to consciously launch academic programmes in the universities, improve the conditions of our archives and manuscripts to encourage the study of Sanskrit and Indian languages and preserve them. We also need more archival material for research. Only then will a systematic study of indigenous historical knowledge can be promoted.

I am most grateful to you for having taken time and encourage this workshop.

Thank you.

Keynote Address by Shri Shivshankar Menon, National Security Advisor

October 18, 2012

It is customary on such occasions to say how delighted one is to come to a meeting and how appropriate its subject is. Today, for once, I mean it in full measure. I am truly delighted to be here at the workshop on Kautilya organised by the IDSA. I must congratulate Director Arvind Gupta on this initiative. I have three reasons to be so delighted. You forced me to read Kautilya again, and that gave me great pleasure. Secondly, the conference enables us to reconnect with the rich Indian tradition of strategic thought. And thirdly, it could contribute to the evolution of our own strategic vocabulary and thought.

Let me expand on that.

1. On Reading Kautilya Again

The *Arthashastra* meets one essential criterion for a great book. It bears reading again and again. Every time you read it you learn something new and find a new way of looking at events. But it is a very different sort of text from the *Bhagwadgita*. This is not a book that you keep on your bedside table and turn to for daily inspiration. This is a serious manual on statecraft, on how to run a state, informed by a higher purpose (or *dharma*), clear and precise in its prescriptions, the result of practical experience of running a state. It is not just a normative text but a realist description of the art of running a state.

Reading the text again now, I was struck by how evidently Kautilya himself (if indeed the author of the *Arthashastra* was one man and not a historical composite) is clearly the product of centuries of evolved strategic thinking. He cites several previous authorities' differing views on many issues. Bharadvaja, Vishalaksha, Parasara, Pisuna and others are mentioned often. Kautilya argues with them, while presenting their views before his own. Sadly, what we know of many of them is limited to what Kautilya tells us.

Equally, Kautilya's is only one voice, and the *Arthashastra* is probably meant to be a normative text, describing how the state should work. Ashoka's imagining of the state's place in the world, judging by his inscriptions, and his practice do not bear out what the *Arthashastra* says. Other Indian texts have different points of view, for instance the Buddhist Nikaya texts, on statecraft and defence. The *Arthashastra* and Kautilya are therefore one of several approaches to statecraft in ancient India. It is also a text of its time and place, Mauryan to Gupta administration, and should be read as such.

I was also struck by the fact that Kautilya's is more than just a power maximisation or internal dominance strategy for a state. He has an almost modern sense of the higher purpose of the state, and of the limits of power.

2. Reconnecting with Indian Strategic Thought

We are afflicted with neglect of our pre-modern histories, and many of us believe orientalist caricatures of India. India's supposedly incoherent strategic approach is actually a colonial construct, as is the idea of Indians somehow forgetting their own history and needing to be taught it by Westerners who retrieved it. The version that they "retrieved" was a construct that was useful to perpetuate colonial rule and, after independence, to induce self-doubt and a willingness to follow.

Reading Kautilya and the other indigenous texts is one way to give the lie to these theories.

The other is to consider strategic practice in India over the ages. One only has to think of the *Mahabharata* (our own Warring States period slightly later), the histories of the Deccan, Kerala, and Bundelkhand in medieval times (to pick a few examples at random) and what we have undergone in the sixty-five years since independence, to see continuity in Indian strategic practice. Fortunately younger Indian historians are now working on these subjects with unblinkered minds. I have just read a book by Jayashree Vivekanandan called *Interrogating International Relations* (Routledge, 2011) which analyses Mughal grand strategy. It strengthened my faith that our scholarly tradition is alive.

But as a general rule, today our theory has yet to catch up with our rich historical praxis.

Reading Kautilya (and other texts like the *Shantiparva* of the *Mahabharata*) one is reminded that this was not always so. One is also reminded of the rich experience in our tradition of multipolarity, of asymmetries in the distribution of power, of debate on the purposes of power (where *dharma* is defined), of the utility of force, and of several other issues with contemporary resonance. In many ways, it is India's historical experience of poly-centric multi-state systems, plurality, and of the omni-directional diplomacy and relativistic statecraft that it produced, that is closer to the world we see today. (In contrast, the single-sovereign, universalist, and hierarchical statecraft and diplomacy of traditional China is easier to explain and attractive in its simplicity but fundamentally different.)

Let me be clear. I am not trying to idealise the Indian past. There is a risk here that the analytic tradition becomes the historical tradition, that we confuse cause and effect, and that imageries become the reality that they were intended to reflect. All I am saying is that some of the problems in IR and strategic studies that we think we are dealing with for the first time have been considered by great minds in India before. We are the poorer for ignoring them. We can, instead, use the past to learn ways of thinking about these problems, improving our mental discipline, as it were.

Besides, states behave in ways that cannot be entirely explained by rational calculation or logic. (If they were they would be predictable.)

Studying strategic traditions and cultures gives us a better understanding of why this is so. And where better to start than with oneself. A little self-awareness cannot hurt.

Let me give you an example of what I mean. When we in India call for a plural, inclusive and open security architecture in the Indo-Pacific we are well within a tradition and culture of thought which was relativistic, idea driven and omni-directional. Other traditions, which are more hierarchical, claiming universal validity, find these ideas hard to understand. (And we are shocked when they do not espouse what to us are our eminently sensible views!) Friends tell me that Chola, Pandyan and Oriya manuscripts and inscriptions are early examples of what the free flow of goods, ideas and people could achieve - the ancient version of the open, inclusive architecture that we speak of today.

3. Creating our Own Modern Strategic Vocabulary

Some of you will groan and say, "There he goes again on his hobby horse." But let me explain why this is important.

To be honest among ourselves, much of what passes for strategic thinking in India today is derivative, using concepts, doctrines and a vocabulary derived from other cultures, times, places and conditions. This is why, with a few honourable exceptions like the home-grown nuclear doctrine, it fails to serve our needs, impact policy, or to find a place in domestic and international discourse.

Jawaharlal Nehru made a beginning towards creating modern Indian strategic thought. But his work was incomplete, even though it was taken forward and developed by others like K. Subrahmaniam. Besides, the world has evolved rapidly since Nehru's time.

There is also no question that we live in a world that is different from Kautilya's in terms of technology and experience. But human responses are still similar, as is the behaviour of the states that humans create and run. That is why reading Kautilya helps us by broadening our vision on issues of strategy.

It will, naturally, take time and practice for us to develop our own strategic vocabulary and doctrines. This will require patience, but must be done if India is to truly seek the broadest possible degree of strategic autonomy. After all autonomy begins in the mind. As I said earlier, fortunately the younger generation of Indian scholars shows signs of doing the necessary work and are thinking for themselves.

Strategic doctrines and cultures are not built in a day. I was, therefore, happy to see that this workshop is part of a broader Indigenous Historical Knowledge project by the IDSA. May I also suggest that this workshop be the first of a series that builds upon the beginning that you are making here? I assume that future workshops and work in the project on Indigenous Historical Knowledge will also cover other Indian thinkers and themes.

With these words, let me wish you and your workshop every success.

About the Contributors

1. Ambassador Shivshankar Menon was the National Security Advisor to the Prime Minister of India from 2010-2014 and Foreign Secretary of India from 2006 to 2009. He has served as Ambassador and High Commissioner to Israel, Sri Lanka, China and Pakistan. He was also seconded to the Department of Atomic Energy in the early eighties and was a member of the Atomic Energy Commission 2008-14. His professional experience was concentrated on India's neighbours, atomic energy and disarmament, and India's relations with the major powers. Menon speaks Chinese and some German. He has an MA degree in History with specialisation in Ancient India.
2. Dr. Arvind Gupta is the Deputy National Security Adviser at the National Security Council Secretariat, Government of India. Earlier, he was the Director General of the Institute for Defence Studies and Analyses (IDSA), New Delhi, from 2012-14.
3. Dr. S. Kalyanaraman is a Research Fellow at the Institute for Defence Studies and Analyses (IDSA), New Delhi.
4. Ambasador A.N.D. Haksar is a retired Indian diplomat and a well-known translator of Sanskrit classics, of which he has rendered a wide cross section into English for modern reading.
5. Group Captain Sachin More is a serving officer in the Indian Air Force. He has written a monograph titled "*Arthasastra*: Lessons for the Contemporary Security Environment with South Asia as a Case Study."

6. Wing Commander G. Adityakiran was Instructor, Defence Service Staff College, Wellington, Tamil Nadu, India. He is now on active service in the field.

7. Dr. Krishnendu Ray is an Associate Professor in the Department of Ancient Indian History & Culture, University of Calcutta.

8. Mr. Tarun Kumar is a doctoral candidate in the University of Delhi and also teaches Political Science at Zakir Hussain College affiliated to the same.

9. Dr. Deepshikha Shahi is an Assistant Professor in the Janki Devi Memorial College, University of Delhi. She is also associated with International Democracy Watch, Italy.

10. Group Captain Vinay Vittal was posted at Air Headquarters, New Delhi. He is now on active service in the field.

11. Colonel Pradeep Kumar Gautam (Retd.) is currently a Research Fellow at the Institute for Defence Studies and Analyses (IDSA), New Delhi and convener of the workshops and seminars with regard to the Indigenous Historical Knowledge Project.

12. Mr. Jean Langlois-Berthelot was formerly an intern with the Institute for Defence Studies and Analyses (IDSA), New Delhi. He has done his M.A. in East Asian Studies from the National School of Advanced Research, Paris.

13. Dr. Saurabh Mishra is a Research Assistant at the Institute for Defence Studies and Analyses (IDSA), New Delhi.

1

Arthashastra, Diplomatic History and the Study of International Relations in India

S. Kalyanaraman

There are three main reasons Kautilya's *Arthashastra* must be studied. First, it is the earliest treatise on statecraft written anywhere in the world and being Indian in origin there is a need to celebrate this heritage by providing it a prominent place in the Indian discourse on International Relations. Second, the *Arthashastra* continues to be relevant because of the key insights it provides about the enduring nature of the state and of the inter-state system as well as because of the framework of thought and action it prescribes for states to navigate through this system. Three of these insights and the prescriptions that follow from them are particularly important:

1) The state is based on power backed by legitimacy, and consequently there is a need for constant efforts to enhance both its power and legitimacy;
2) The state ceaselessly engages in the pursuit of wealth and power and self-aggrandisement in an anarchic inter-state system in which *matsyanyaya* (the concept of big fish swallowing smaller fish) prevails and frequent wars and struggles for supremacy occur; and,

3) The doctrine of *mandala* provides both a categorisation of states and their inter-relationships as well as prescriptions on how to exploit this matrix to one's advantage.

The third and even more important reason for studying the *Arthashastra* is to provide a boost for the discipline of International Relations in India, a discipline that is widely acknowledged as continuing to wallow on the margins of the global discourse in this field. A number of factors have been identified for the poor state of the International Relations discipline in India.[1] For one, the study of International Relations in India is limited to contemporary affairs dating back to India's independence and the years since the end of the Second World War. This focus on contemporary and current affairs imposes serious limitations in terms of openly available information given the extreme secrecy that the government perseveres to maintain over issues that continue to have repercussions for its conduct of foreign, defence and security policies. Secondly, from its inception, the field of International Relations in India has been heavily skewed in favour of Area Studies with an emphasis upon bilateral relations and developments within individual countries or a region. As a result, the field of International Relations in India has largely come to be equated with Area Studies that too with an emphasis upon current and contemporary affairs.[2] This is, however, not to mean that other sub-disciplines and functional areas are completely neglected. Jawaharlal Nehru University (JNU), New Delhi, for instance, has vibrant programmes on arms control and disarmament, diplomacy, international economics, international law, international organisation and international politics and theory. A third important factor for the unsatisfactory nature of the discipline has been the "resistance to theory" and indeed its denigration, which has left the discipline "without a sense of self-reflexiveness, that is, systematic and conscious reflection on the conduct and goals of inquiry."[3]

While each of the above factors has indeed played a significant role in constraining the vibrancy of the discipline of International Relations in India, another equally critical factor has been the complete neglect of India's diplomatic history; a history that dates back at least 2500 years to the era of the 16 oligarchies and monarchies known as the *mahajanapada*, and a history which includes the rise and fall of great empires as well as the operation of a vibrant inter-state system during the interregnums between these empires. This rich history has not only been completely ignored in the study of International Relations in India, but even premier social science centres like JNU's Centre for Historical Studies, for instance, have consciously limited their focus to social and economic history.

In contrast, the study of International Relations elsewhere in the world, and particularly in the Anglosphere which has attained and continues to retain hegemonic status in the discipline, begins with the diplomatic history of the ancient Greek city-state system, traverses through the rise and fall of the Roman Empire, then jumps to the rise of European states and the operation and global expansion of the European international system, before coming to the Cold War and its aftermath. For instance, the course on Grand Strategy at Yale University includes the following topics: Sun Tzu's *The Art of War*, Thucydides' *History of the Peloponnesian War*, Machiavelli's *The Prince*, the rise and fall of the Roman Empire, the ideas of Immanuel Kant, the diplomatic craft of Prince Metternich, Clausewitz's *On War*, Bismarck and the rise of Germany, the rise of the United States, the geopolitics of imperial, democratic and authoritarian states in the modern era, and finally the Cold War and its end.

Given this sheer breadth in scope of the study of diplomatic history as an integral part of International Relations in the Anglosphere and the serious engagement of scholars from these countries in the development of International Relations theory, it is but natural that the Western discourse has attained a hegemonic position in the field. If the Indian discourse is to carve out a niche for itself in the International Relations firmament, Indian scholars have to necessarily immerse themselves in studying India's own experience of war, diplomacy and statecraft as practised by the great Indian empires and various kingdoms and dynasties over the last 2500 years. Of course, there may be serious constraints in studying ancient Indian diplomatic history in particular because of the absence of written Indian records except for Ashoka's edicts and the unreliable nature of what Greek sources are available. But definitely these constraints do not apply to later historical periods.

It is within this broader focus upon the diplomatic history of pre-1947 India that the study of ancient Indian treatises such as the *Arthashastra* as well as many other classical texts needs to be located. Studying this history will enrich the Indian discourse in International Relations including by providing a laboratory to test and enrich the concepts and theories postulated both by contemporary scholars as well as by classical Indian thinkers like Kautilya. And ultimately, a more rigorous Indian discourse in International Relations would enrich collective understanding and help India navigate through the shoals of international politics. After all, the key question in the study of International Relations has never been 'what should we know?' but instead 'what should we do?' to deal with the security challenges and foreign policy predicaments that countries face.[4]

NOTES

1. For a critical appraisal of the state of the discipline in India and the problems plaguing it, see the several articles in the special issue of *International Studies*, 46 (1) & (2), 2009.
2. A.P. Rana and K.P. Misra, "Communicative Discourse and Community in International Relations Studies in India: A Critique," in Kanti Bajpai and Siddharth Mallavarapu (eds.), *International Relations in India: Bringing Theory Back Home,* Orient Longman, New Delhi, 2005, pp. 74-77; also see, Varun Sahni, "The Fallacies and Flaws of Area Studies in India," in *International Studies*, 46 (1) & (2), 2009, pp. 49-68.
3. Kanti Bajpai, "International Studies in India: Bringing Theory (Back) Home," in Kanti Bajpai and Siddharth Mallavarapu (eds.), *International Relations in India: Bringing Theory Back Home,* Orient Longman, New Delhi, 2005, p. 25.
4. Stanley Hoffmann, "An American Social Science: International Relations," in *Daedalus*, 106 (3), Summer 1977, p. 58.

2

A Post-Kautilya View of Diplomacy: The *Nitisara* of Kamandaki

A.N.D. Haksar

The name Kautilya has become iconic in independent India, a symbol of our own ancient science of government. This is evident from prominent place names like Kautilya Marg and Chanakyapuri in the national capital and the titles of several Indian institutions devoted to political studies today. The repute of the *Kautiliya Arthashastra* as a fount of these studies has further grown with continued academic research about it. But this can perhaps tend to overshadow other less known or distinguished ancient works which also form a part of our rich traditional literature on governance and policy that, as a whole, is categorised generally with the word *niti,* or guidance and political wisdom. This aspect also needs bearing in mind during discussions.

The *Arthashastra* of Kautilya is a part of this age-old literature, and certainly the most detailed and seminal work in it so far known. It begins with a statement that it was prepared after reviewing the *Arthashastras* taught by earlier teachers. While any such older texts are yet to be located and identified definitely, those of several *niti* works which followed Kautilya's classic are extant and available. Of them, 13 have been detailed by Winternitz in his well known history.[1] They stretch over an approximate 1000 year period from the 7th to the 17th centuries, and across venues ranging from present day Kerala to Kashmir and Gujarat to Bihar. It would thus appear that the composition and study of *niti* literature in Sanskrit has a long history in this country. Such works may be of variable quality but at least some of them are significant and deserve more attention than they have so far received.

One such work is the *Nitisara* of Kamandaki considered here. Let me begin on a personal note about how I came to know of it. It was perhaps the result of a conjunction between a long experience in diplomacy and a more recent interest in translating Sanskrit classics. I first read about Kamandaki while translating the *Dasa Kumara Charitam* of Dandin.[2] That famous classical critic and author mentions the works of both Kautilya and Kamandaki while describing the education of a prince.[3] Writing at another place on the elements of governance, he uses language which his commentator puts into context with a quote from the *Nitisara*.[4] Later, while translating the *Hitopadesa* of Narayana, I discovered that this celebrated work quotes nearly 90 verses from the *Nitisara*, mainly on political theory, including 20 which describe 16 types of peace treaties.[5]

This led me eventually to the *Nitisara* itself. It is a substantial Sanskrit work, comprising 1192 verses grouped into 20 chapters, some with multiple subject headings which total 37 altogether. These include the traditional branches of learning, the established social order, the state, its constituents and preservation, the *mandala* theory on inter-state relations, various types of policy, war and peace, diplomacy and intelligence, military organisation, and defects to avoid. The work's dating remains debatable, but it is obviously earlier than those of the 7th century Dandin and the 10th century Narayana which I have already mentioned. Details of its author, Kamandaki, are also still untraced. But this work was readily available during the period of the British East India Company, and was first published with the title *The Elements of Polity* by the Asiatic Society in 1849.[6] The *Arthashastra*, it is worth remembering, was located and published in British India only 60 years later. It was of course known and lauded in Indian tradition since much before, including by Kamandaki. Here is a rough translation of what the latter says in his opening verses, where he refers to Kautilya by that luminary's less well known third name.

"Salutations to the wise and learned Vishnugupta, who extracted the nectar of *niti* from the ocean of the *Arthashastras*. The mighty Nandas were uprooted and brought down by his tactics, like a hill by a flaming thunderbolt, and the godlike power of his advice alone secured the earth for King Chandragupta. Having studied the work of that clear-minded master, out of our love for the science of governance and our wish to condense it in a volume, we here indicate the views of experts in that science on the acquisition and protection of a land by a ruler."[7]

It is quite clear from these verses that Kamandaki's *Nitisara* has acknowledged its inspiration from the *Arthashastra* of Kautilya. The mutual relation of the two works has received divergent comments from eminent modern Sanskritists. Keith called *Nitisara* "merely a redaction of the *Arthashastra*."[8] Winternitz considered that it "shows significant deviations that prove the author had (also) utilised some other sources."[9] A comparative analysis of the two texts, and some other texts of the same category, may help to further trace the indigenous development of political theory in India, and could perhaps be a project for due consideration. Such a project could provide additional sources for present knowledge on this subject, including for a glossary of technical terms for international affairs.

My observations here are confined to a single aspect of the *Nitisara* which may be of interest for our present diplomatic studies and training. This is its account of the role of an ambassador or envoy as then seen. The subject has also been covered by Kautilya, but here it is perhaps treated in more detail. It is contained in the *Nitisara*'s chapter 13. The background, further indicated in its chapter 8 on the *mandala* system, presupposes broadly that all states have and need to take account of threat perceptions from other political entities. It is in this background that the work considers the diplomat's role. Here is a broad retelling of what is said in its concerned verses.[10]

After due consultation with experienced advisers, writes Kamandaki, a wise ruler sends with their approval a qualified envoy to the state with which action is contemplated. A royal envoy should be a bold and mature person. He should be eloquent, have a good memory, be versed in both political and military matters, and fully experienced in his functions. There are three categories of envoys in a descending order of authority: with full powers of negotiation, with limited powers as specified, and those who just convey messages.

The ambassador, Kamandaki continues, goes to his destination and negotiates on the basis of his master's brief with due thought to the other side's reply and counter-replies. He cultivates the friendship of people on the frontier and in the forests to understand the river and land routes for the success of his forces. He should not enter the other side's city or assembly unannounced, but wait for due permission before doing so. He should apprise himself of that state's resources and defences, its vulnerabilities and allies, its finances and military power.

Even if threatened, an envoy should communicate his message as directed, and assess the other side's reactions, quietly promoting any differences within it, but without admitting to any inadequacy in his own side. Even if questioned, he should not speak about his side's shortcomings, saying only 'everything is known to you', and praising the other ruler's nobility, resources and deeds. But, on the pretext of teaching, learning and the arts, the envoy can cultivate those having interests in both sides, so that he may identify people who could, if needed, be incited against their ruler. Such people can be told about his own master's beneficial qualities. Meanwhile he should maintain secret contacts with his side's agents in hermitages and places of pilgrimage.

An envoy should tolerate abuse, and himself avoid sexual attraction, anger and bad company. Concealing his own feelings while ascertaining those of the other side, he should keep away from women and drink, and always sleep alone: for personal feelings can get exposed in drunken or loving talk. The wise envoy will not let himself be upset or exhausted in accomplishing his work, but move only at the right time, meanwhile collecting information with various inducements. Seeking the benefit of his side, he will look for advantages of time and space so that they are not outwitted by the other. If the latter defers his moves, he will weigh the reasons for it. And when the time is ripe for action, he will go back and report to his master or send special messages while staying in position.

Identification of the enemy's enemy; alienation of his friends and associates; knowledge about his financial and military strength; winning over his disaffected officers; and securing information about his topography for troop movements: these are said to be an envoy's duties. It is only through his ambassador that a ruler may learn of the enemy state's intentions. In his own interest, however, he also needs to keep himself informed of the activities of the other side's ambassador.

Such is the *Nitisara* account of the ambassador's role. It is of course rather limited in terms of the ever growing range of diplomatic duties today. But it is not irrelevant, even now, to some basic requirements for discharging such duties in relations between states. To that extent it deserves note in present studies of the subject. So do other sections of Kamandaki's treatise, dealing with war and peace, defence, intelligence and other items which have been mentioned but not detailed in this paper. Such studies could enable comparison of his appraisals with those of Kautilya, perhaps a millennium earlier, and also shed light on the then Indian political backgrounds in which they were respectively made.

From a modern perspective, it may appear that the emphasis in a work like the *Nitisara* is almost only on state institutions and not the people. That also is not entirely correct as would be seen from its introductory verses and its chapter 5 on the ruler and the dependents. Though outside the scope of this article on diplomatic practice, let me conclude with a quote from that chapter to give a broader idea of Kamandaki's work.

"The people's fears are five-fold: from state officials, from criminals, from external enemies, from those dear to the ruler, and from the ruler's own greed. Removing these five, the ruler earns benefits in due time, and also augments his triple store of virtue, wealth and pleasure".[11]

NOTES

1. M. Winternitz, *History of Indian Literature*, Vol. III (tr. S. Jha), Motilal Banarsidass, Delhi, 1963, pp. 634-53.
2. A.N.D. Haksar (tr.), *Tales of the Ten Princes*, Penguin Books, Delhi, 1995.
3. *Ibid.,* p. 17 and note 1.6.
4. *Ibid.*, note 13.14.
5. A.N.D. Haksar (tr.), *Hitopadesa*, Penguin Books, Delhi, 1998, p. xiii.
6. S.K. Mitra (ed.), *The Nitisara by Kamandaki*, The Asiatic Society, Calcutta, 1982.

7. *Ibid.*, p.3, *Nitisara*, vv.1.4-6.
8. A.B. Keith, A *History of Sanskrit Literature*, Oxford University Press, London, 1920, p. 462.
9. M. Winternitz (ed.), note 1, p. 635.
10. S.K. Mitra (ed.), note 6, pp. 258-66, *Nitisara,* vv.13. 1-24.
11. S.K. Mitra (ed.), note 6, p. 123, *Nitisara*, vv.5.82-3.

3

Kautilya on State Fragility in Contemporary Security Environment

Sachin More

Arthashastra has invoked serious academic debate in the fields of Economics, Management, Justice and Foreign Affairs. However, its treatment on matters concerning contemporary security issues is largely unexplored. The prescriptive teachings of Kautilya are underpinned with his deeper understanding of the factors that promote stability in a state and through this stability progress in the wider sense. *Arthashastra*, therefore, adds value to the state, the society and the individual. Flowing from this fundamental wisdom, Kautilya builds on the state's strengths and provides courses of action that its policy makers can adopt, when faced with situations in the security and foreign policy domain. This paper is an attempt to situate the *Arthashastra* in the modern age, to stimulate interest in the enduring topics it addresses; and offers a fresh perspective through an alternate strategic discourse.

The paper assumes a working knowledge of the models of *mandala*, *sadgunyas*, *upayas* and *prakritis* as given in the *Arthashastra*. The paper begins by developing an understanding of the contemporary security environment in the post cold war world. The current world understanding of statehood is then examined through the lens of the *Arthashastra* and the concept of *prakritis* to determine the efficacy of utilising Kautilyan frameworks to model state behavior. The choices that *sadgunyas* offer are analysed within the context of the *Mandala* framework that a state can adopt. With a whole system approach, the result that the adopted *sadgunyas* have on *prakritis* is then understood and compared with the ideal *prakritis* that are provided by Kautilya. The deviation from the ideal state of *prakritis* is an imbalance which determines the 'fragility' or lack of stability in that state. Through a counterfactual analysis, lack of stability can be ascertained through the non-adherence to the courses of action proposed by Kautilya. Thus, the state of the security environment in the present information rich globalised contemporary world can be seen through the lens of the *Arthashastra*.

Contemporary Security Environment

The contemporary security environment is marked by trans-national terrorism and criminality intertwined within economic and informational domains, which blur the conventionally understood models of security of the cold war era.[1] The informational revolution has accelerated the process of globalisation and has not permitted the traditionally understood security models to keep pace with the rapidly evolving threats of non-state actors; who thrive in ungoverned fragile spaces. The traditional state response to such threats, much epitomised in the 'Global War on Terror' has further widened this gap.

Commenting on the scale and scope of contemporary security issues, Hanlon contends that in the contemporary environment, a majority of the world's states can be classified as weak, failing, or failed.[2] She notes that, "more than half of the world's population lives in fragile states, which are likely to be among the preponderant sources of instability, conflict, and war over the next decade or two, at the very least. These states provide the conditions for the incubation and maturation of hundreds of armed groups to include insurgents, terrorists, militias and criminal organisations."[3] The proliferation of new states, in the latter part of the 20th century, has further raised huge challenges of organisation and governance.[4]

In search for a viable political structure, these states show the classic signs of weakening from within and the resultant economic inequity is exacerbated under the prevalent climate of globalisation. The fragility in such states creates permissive spaces; which allow terror groups the freedom to operate in the increasingly economically inter-twined world. The inability of the fragile states to address ungoverned spaces within their territory makes them liable to intervention from stronger states, challenging their statehood and sovereignty. The fragile states are here to coexist with the relatively stable states and their struggles and bids to achieve parity rhymes completely with the tensions experienced in the warring states of the *Arthashastra*.

Arthashastra: Conception of Statehood and Security

The aspects that make a state stable have been discussed by Kautilya, who in his treatise gave a comprehensive framework of the constituents or *prakritis* of a state.[5] There are seven *prakritis*, which constitute the seven pillars on which the state can be considered to stand strong; and which provide a base for attempting expansion and progress. Thus, a weakness in any one would impact adversely on the ability of the state to function effectively and it would make the state fragile.[6] To draw a modern analogy, Buzan states that there are three component parts of a state, which are interlinked—'the idea of a state, the physical base of a state and the institutional expression of a state'.[7] To discuss these further:

(a) Buzan claims that a state without a binding idea might be so disadvantaged as to be unable to sustain its existence in a competitive international system.[8] The idea that binds the Mauryan Empire is that of a balanced state, which seeks a balance of the triad of *artha-dharma-kama* and was represented through a capable leadership performing the King's duty.

(b) Buzan says that 'the physical base of the state comprises its population and territory, including all of its natural resources and manmade wealth contained within its borders'.[9] The *janapada* and *durg* are the manifestations of the physical essence of the Kautilyan state.

(c) The institutions, which comprise the entire machinery of government, form the third pillar in this overarching framework; and are present as *amatya* in the *Arthashastra*. Buzan and Waltz emphasise that a weakness in the idea and institutions of a state, leads to a weaker state.[10] These arguments resonate with the order of priorities Kautilya puts in *prakritis,* laying emphasis on a strong leadership and a capable set of ministers to effectively harness the human and natural resources available to the state.

A representation of these is as placed in figure 1 given below, which depicts the prioritisation of the seven *prakritis* in the reducing order of priority starting with the leader and ending with the alliance.[11] The centrality of progress depicted through the King's duty or '*rajdharma*' which is akin to a social contract is represented through the triad of *rakshana* (protection), *palana* (welfare) and *yogakshema* (rule of law).[12] The obligation to perform this social contract grants legitimacy to the ruler to exercise control over the state.

Figure 1

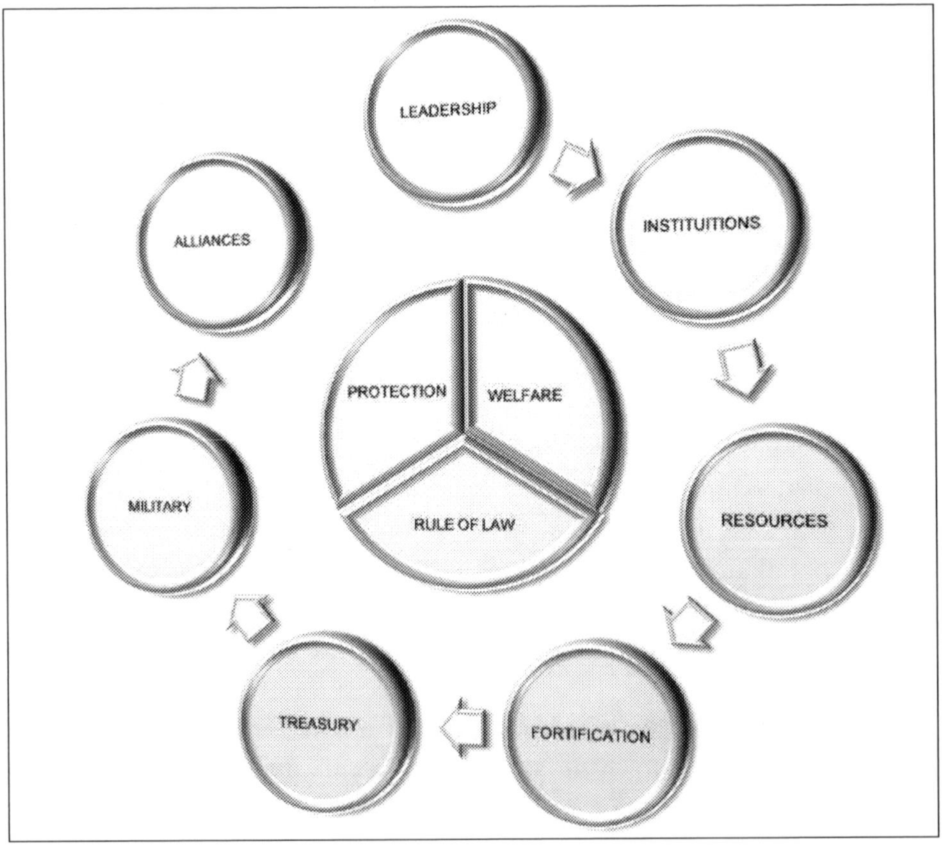

This representation shows that Kautilya's *prakritis* go on to include the treasury, military forces and alliances in the *Arthashastra's* comprehensive discourse on national power that links the macro to the micro level and adds additional dimensions to Buzan's conception of the state. In particular, the addition of *mitra* or alliances to this equation, allows the Kautilyan state to extend the national power through the capacities and capabilities that the allies offer, and reflects the reality in the world politics as seen today; wherein even stronger states seek alliances to strengthen their powerbase without diluting own capabilities or sovereignty. The viability of alliances in the national conception of power has thus been an accepted norm in all modern progressive states that understand the need to engage with states with mutually beneficial priorities to achieve security that permits the achievement of progress. At this juncture, it is necessary to emphasise that Kautilya's advice is suitable not only for nation building, stability and advancement, but also to explore how certain policies that are contrary to fundamental laws of statecraft as defined by Kautilya have a resultant outcome of decline.

A Whole System Approach

To develop a wholesome understanding of the phenomena that *Arthashastra* delves into, it is essential to capture the entire spectrum of issues and glean out the inter-linkages that exist between the elements of internal and external policies of the state. Kautilya's conceptualisation of inter-state relations was based on the foundations of competitive advantage in an anarchic world. *Arthashastra's* paradigms for inter-state relations through the construct of the *mandala* theory and classification of the choice of policies through *sadgunyas* and *upayas* were meant to provide the state the relative advantage to achieve progress. While the health of the *prakritis* provides a barometer of internal happiness and progress, the external counter balance achieved within the *mandala* is essential to sustain it and is based on the choices made by the state. For achieving success in the *mandala* system, Kautilya offers *sadgunya* for the *vijigishu* to apply to the constituent elements of his circle of states.[13]

Rangarajan clarifies that the conqueror is not necessarily 'a good king' and, correspondingly, the enemy 'a bad king'. The advice can be equally applied to both kings.[14] Kautilya's use of the word *Vijigishu* is for purely theoretical purposes as he gives sufficient advice to a weak king to pursue against a strong king.[15] Through this evidence, the application of the *Arthashastra's* theories can be done to all states, regardless of their policies and can be a useful tool to model state behaviour and understand motivations, behaviour and outcomes. The choices within the *sadgunyas* are depicted in figure 2 to show their rclative utility in the modern understanding of the options available to a state within the security spectrum from complete peace through shades of green and red to complete war.

Figure 2

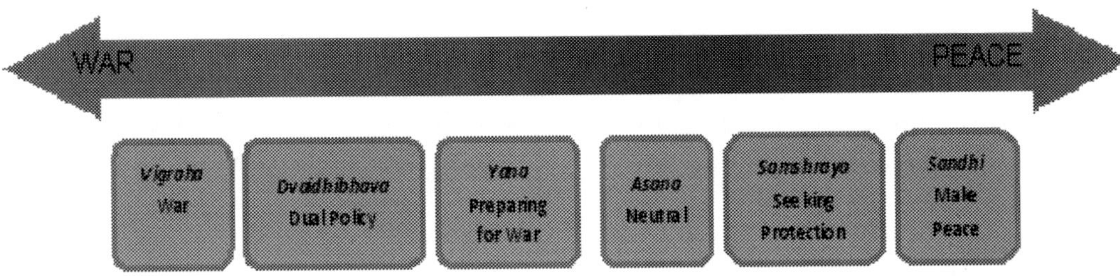

Kautilya makes a very important contribution when he juxtaposes the temporal domain with the *sadgunyas*. Boesche calls this as the 'Pendulum theory of history' in which Kautilya depicts the kingdom passing through three phases—decline, stability and advancement.[16] Kautilya says that when in decline, make peace, when prospering, make war, if equal in strength, remain neutral, depleted in power, seek shelter, with help, seek dual policy and when blessed with excellence, prepare for war.[17] He then goes on to highlight the importance of the policies adopted by the state on its endeavours and links this to the outcome, which may be progress, stability or decline. He says that *vyasanas* or calamities contribute to decline and they can be attributed to human policies or natural calamities.[18] Boesche comments that Kautilya's science of politics can assist in "prolonging the state of advancement, but mistakes and natural calamities always occur to transport a kingdom back from advancement to decline."[19] While he attributes policy making to good or bad outcomes, he attributes 'divine' intervention for good fortune and misfortune. This evidence reveals that by differentiating between stochastic and deterministic events,[20] Kautilya was able to refine *Arthashastra* and provide well reasoned solutions for the dynamic problems in statecraft.

To apply the Kautilyan model in the modern security context, Rangarajan's analysis is useful, "Kautilya uses four devices to derive practical advice for specific situations from his essential theoretical concepts. These are: relative power, deviations from the ideal, classification of type of motivation, and the influence of the intangible and the unpredictable."[21] Kautilya places great emphasis on relative power in a bilateral relation to support a course of action.[22] Kautilya warns that power is not constant over time and advises a course of action based on deviations by factoring the variations in power on a temporal frame.[23] The sub classification of types of neighbours, types of allies and types of vassals permits an analysis of the motives of the actors and allows a reasoned response through the models that Kautilya proposes.[24] Kautilya brings clarity on tangible factors when he brings out the importance of the power of good command, analysis and judgement; and on unpredictable factors, which are attributed to acts of god outside human control.[25]

Sihag contends that, "Kautilya invariably applied cost-benefit analysis to every undertaking, including waging a war. But he was against applying the usual cost-benefit analysis to the provision of national security, which he argued was too fundamental to be decided by such calculations. According to him, a nation had to match or exceed the power of her potential adversary, since national security depended only on relative power."[26] In this way, this paper notes that Kautilya makes a clear distinction between war as a national necessity for survival, which does not rely on cost-benefit analysis, and the present day use of war as a matter of choice by the western world, where at a certain stage the cost-benefit analysis comes into play, due to the very nature of wars that the West engages in. This is reflected in the desire of the West to effect a withdrawal from Afghanistan without addressing the root cause of instability as it does not affect the West directly. With the analyses that Sihag provides, it emerges that the use of *sadgunya* by a state has to be done within a temporal and calculated framework, where the cost-benefit analysis is situated depending on the type of threat to national security. There is undoubtedly a need for a whole system approach while seeking deeper understanding of the way

Figure 3

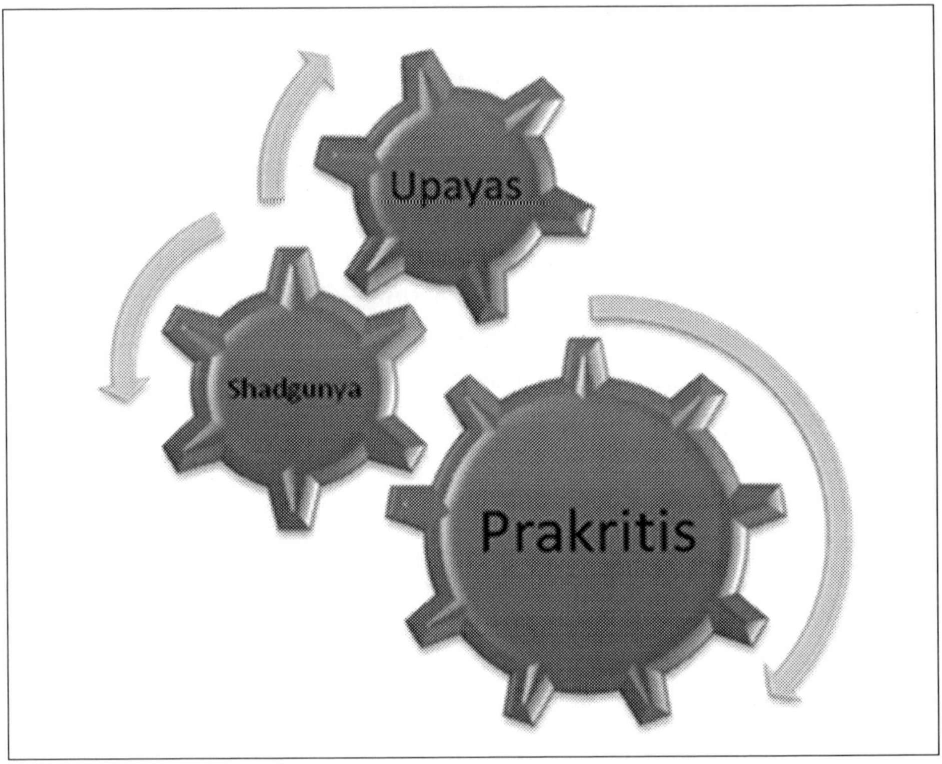

the inter-linkages of various models that Kautilya prescribes, metaphorically represented in Figure 3.

Contemporary Analysis

The paper now seeks to explore the intrinsic linkage of the choice of *sadgunyas* within the *mandalas* to the health of the *prakritis*. The duty of the King is to provide the right atmosphere to his subject to achieve progress. The conflicts in the current era are of prolonged nature, with loosely defined ends. Such conflicts make demands which are unsustainable and promote depletion of the *prakritis*. This does not allow the *prakritis* to be prioritised in the order proposed by Kautilya. This study aims at understanding this with a whole system approach, joining the dots and connecting the patterns to glean out the inter-linkages. A deeper analysis is thus possible with this approach. The use of *sadgunyas* to form policies within the *mandala* has a direct impact on the *prakritis* and this can be gleaned when the entire process is played out to see the inter-linkages.

The order of priority of various constituents elements of the state have been described by Kautilya. They are in natural order of priority for progress and when the order is disturbed, there is likely to be a decline of the state. The *vyasanas* are the prime contributors in reversing the trend of progress. The *vyasanas* have been attributed to both man-made and natural consequences. Kautilya's prescriptions have shown that he understood the relevance of deterministic and stochastic variables; and by addressing them, he was able to provide a reasoned advice which increased the probability of success. However, the order of priority is not rigid and Kautilya provides exceptions to permit deviations for specific circumstances. This is specifically applicable when the aspect of time is superimposed on the choice of *sadgunyas* and *upayas*.

This paper attempts to enliven the whole system approach through a real world case study of the state of Pakistan. The choice of Pakistan for case study is based on the current discourse on the fragility that this state faces in the contemporary security environment. The whole system approach becomes amply clear through a case study of Pakistan and its choice of *sadgunyas vis-a-vis* India. In the state of Pakistan, the long term perception of insecurity from India has shaped its choices in its *mandala.* Pakistan's need for balancing a conventionally strong India post 1971 war, has led it to adopt a hedging strategy based on alliances,[27] with a prominent role played by the United States, China and Saudi Arabia. Over years, within its strategic calculus, Pakistan has been successful in the context of what its policymakers set out to achieve i.e. strategic parity *vis-a-vis* India.

The effective use of choices within *mandala* theory and innate use of *sadgunyas* and *upayas* juxtaposed with intelligent mix of covert and silent wars has allowed it to exercise a variety of courses of actions in its bid to achieve parity with India. However, while achieving this parity, it needed recourse to an authoritarian form of leadership that imposes the national security criterion on the state without a cost-benefit bias. The authoritarian nature of its leadership (military/civilian) has compromised the fundamental social contract or *rajdharma*, considered essential for the ruler to gain legitimacy. This has in turn come as a heavy cost to its constituent *prakritis*;

affected by human policies and natural calamities, which has led to huge challenges like a depleted treasury, affected the cohesion of its institutions, its ability to harness its own resources, its physical structure and finally the very idea of its statehood.

The effect of realising the wrong prioritisation of the constituent elements of *prakritis* in this case clearly highlights the importance of legitimate leadership and institutions over other constituents and hence validates the prioritisation made by Kautilya. His understanding of inter-state alliances reveals the inherent tensions, risks and opportunities that accompany the choices exercised by states. When the *prakritis* manifest themselves and are counter prioritised, the result is decline that is further sustained by the external policies adopted within the *mandala*.

Impact on Sovereignty

Buzan recognises sovereignty as the "glue that binds the territorial-polity-society package together."[28] He explains that in simple terms, it is self-governance and the ability of a state to provide sufficient capability for sovereignty to be exercised.[29] Buzan also notices that though sovereignty is a contested concept with a problem of interpretation, in practice it is easy to be identified by its absence.[30] Clarifying this, he elaborates, "social units which claim it [sovereignty] must do so openly, and failure to exercise it, or disputes over the right to do so, will usually be evident."[31] Thus, the ability of a state to effectively conduct its affairs without external interference constitutes sovereignty and Kautilya had propounded this very fundamental concept through the treatise.[32] The paper shall examine this through the continuation of the discussion on the case study.

Perceived insecurity from India has made Pakistan to enter alliances that permit it to hedge itself against India. This capability was derived at the cost of permitting foreign hands, overt or covert, to operate from its territory and allowing the US to exercise leverage over its policies. The lack of strong leadership and institutions has allowed an incremental loss of sovereignty; which is assisted by the growing Western appetite to engage upstream. This is especially visible in the contemporary context as the US claims that Pakistan "is unable or unwilling to prevent al Qaeda fighters from hiding and planning future attacks within its borders"; permitting "the

United States (US) use of self-defensive force …[justified] under Article 51 of the United Nations (UN) Charter."[33] The US-Pakistan cooperation today is characterised by its military presence as the US unleashes its 'technological' capabilities through the use of 'drones' against the 'Taliban' and violates the sovereignty of Pakistan with practically no leverage from Pakistan.[34]

The presence of US troops that threaten and use 'kinetic-effects' on Pakistan's territory demonstrates a strong element of coercion from an external power within its own borders, displaying the weakness in the *prakritis*. In effect, though the US action against the Taliban constitutes credible action from a tactical perspective, in real political terms; it raises serious questions about the breach of Pakistan's sovereignty by its intended ally within its designed *mandala*, an action over which it has limited leverage. This reflects the *vyasana* or the calamity that it has had to face for entering an alliance it perceived as a necessity for its survival, but which, from the lens of the US, emerges a war of choice, with the ability to decide on the date of withdrawal.[35]

Seen in the context of the contemporary security environment, an incremental loss of sovereignty due to poor health of *prakritis* leads to a permissive space accorded within the fragile state. Globalisation permits a medium for non-state actors to use this space as the means to achieve their ends, and cause trouble. The importance of information as a tool to achieve dominance was emphasised in every aspect of the state's working in the *Arthashastra*. The ability of non-state actors to circumvent the informational domains of host countries and exploit the relatively ungoverned global spaces further brings into focus the importance that Kautilya attaches to information systems to track the rogue elements of society. Thus the contra-prioritisation of *prakritis* has meant a compromise in both external and internal sovereignty as seen from the case study highlighted above. The whole system approach allows the study of the dynamics of internal and external forces within the prioritisation offered by Kautilya in the *Arthashastra* and proves its timeless validity.

Conclusion

The *Arthashastra* identifies fundamental themes through models and paradigms that have universal validity. The secular and logical tone of its delivery accompanied with empirical leanings is provided by the wide range of detailed deterministic and stochastic possibilities; and thus allows it to be interpreted through modern paradigms. Such models can be detached from discussions involving religion or ideologies and address the root relationships amongst contending issues without a bias. The study also reveals that it is of use in not only analysing and interpreting the ideal set of state policies, but also the flawed state policies and perceptions. The richness of options that Kautilya provides, allows problems to be understood and tackled through informed human decisions. A whole system approach of understanding is recommended in establishing the inter-linkages within the dynamics of the internal and external affairs to establish the root causes of fragility.

NOTES

1. Joseph S. Nye, Jr., and David A. Welch, *Understanding Global Conflict and Cooperation,* Pearson, New Jersey, 2010, p. 289.
2. Querine Hanlon, "State Actors in the 21st Century Security Environment", in *Adapting America's Security Paradigm and Security Agenda,* 7/2011, 1, at http://www.strategycenter.org/wp-content/uploads/2011/07/State-Actors-21st-Century.pdf (Accessed May 15, 2012)
3. *Ibid.*, p. 1.
4. *Ibid.*, pp. 2-3.
5. For a detailed reading of individual *prakriti*s, refer to R.P. Kangle, *The Kautiliya Arthasastra Part II,* Motilal Banarsidass, New Delhi, 2010, pp. 364-367.
6. L.N. Rangarajan, *Kautilya: The Arthashastra,* Penguin Books, New Delhi, 2000, p. 117.
7. Barry Buzan, *People, States and Fear: An Agenda for International Security Studies in the Post Cold War Era,* Harvester Wheatsheaf, London, 1991, p. 65.
8. *Ibid.*, p. 69.
9. *Ibid.*, p. 90.
10. *Ibid.*, p. 97.
11. L.N. Rangarajan, note 6, p. 126.
12. *Ibid.*, p. 15.
13. *Ibid.*, p. 563.
14. *Ibid.*, p. 542.
15. *Ibid.*, p. 550.
16. Roger Boesche, *The First Great Political Realist: Kautilya and His Arthashastra,* Lexington Books, Oxford, 2002, p. 99.
17. R.P. Kangle, note 5, p. 373.
18. L.N. Rangarajan, note 6, p. 122.

19. Roger Boesche, note 16, p. 99.
20. In the study of probability, stochastic events are unpredictable and deterministic events are predictable.
21. L.N. Rangarajan, note 6, p. 543.
22. *Ibid.*, p. 543.
23. *Ibid.*
24. *Ibid.*, p. 544.
25. *Ibid.*
26. Balbir Singh Sihag, "Kautilya on Public goods and taxation", in *History of Political Economy*, 34 (1), 2005, p. 725.
27. A.Z. Hilali, *US-Pakistan Relationship: Soviet Invasion of Afghanistan,* Ashgate Publishing, Aldershot, 2005, p. 36.
28. Barry Buzan, note 7, p. 67.
29. *Ibid.*, 67.
30. *Ibid.*, 67.
31. *Ibid.*, 67,68.
32. R.P. Kangle, note 5, p. 448.
33. Andrew C. Orr, "Unmanned, Unprecedented, and Unresolved: The Status of American Drone Strikes in Pakistan under International Law", in *Cornell International Law Journal*, 44(3), p. 732.
34. Shuja Nawaz, "Drone Attacks inside Pakistan: Wayang or Willing suspension of Disbelief?", in *Georgetown Journal of International Affairs,* Summer/Fall 2011, p. 80.
35. *Ibid.*, p. 81.

4

Kautilya's Pioneering Exposition of Comprehensive National Power in the *Arthashastra*

G. Adityakiran

"Strength is power; happiness is the objective of using power... Welfare of a state depends on an active foreign policy"

—Former Prime Minister P.V. Narasimha Rao[1]

The *Arthashastra* was authored by Kautilya around 300 BC. It was written essentially as a practical treatise on the art of governance. It assumes monarchy to be the normal form of government and is addressed to the king directly. It advises him on administering his state and how he should adjust his foreign policy to the kingdom's best advantage. In both respects—internal administration and foreign relations—the comprehensiveness of its treatment is almost unparalleled.[2] Although Kautilya proposed an elaborate welfare state in domestic politics, something that has been called a socialised monarchy, he proved willing to defend the general good of this monarchy with harsh measures.[3] The *Artha* in the term *Arthashastra* means the sense of territory where men live and seek their material well-being. Thus *Arthashastra* is regarded as the science concerned with the general well-being of the territory wherein its protection (*palana*) and further acquisition (*labha*) become an essential activity.[4] It deals with the science of statecraft, politics, administration and foreign policy. Therefore, we can say that the *Arthashastra* deals with the concept of national power and the art of deploying and furthering it. It is accordingly structured. The declared aim of the *Arthashastra* is that it sets before the *vijigishu*, the conqueror, the goal of conquest of the world and describes ways of attaining that goal.[5]

It is accepted that the *Arthashastra* was the principal tome which helped direct the strategy and statecraft of the Mauryan Empire. Emperor Chandragupta conquered the trans-Indus region in addition to the Magadhan Empire. His son, Emperor Bindusara increased it further to include *Gandhara* and the *Andhras*. His son, Ashoka the Great, established the largest Indian empire encompassing almost the entire Indian sub-continent inclusive of the erstwhile *Gandhara* and south of Bactria. The *Arthashastra* thus laid the foundation for the growth of the Mauryan Empire. Therefore, the *Arthashastra* could provide a conceptual and theoretical framework for understanding national power, relative national power and its characteristic employment towards achieving national objectives. This paper aims to explore the concepts of national power as postulated by Kautilya and incorporate the same in a modern contemporary framework towards defining and maximising Comprehensive National Power (CNP).

The *Arthashastra* was one of the first texts to manifestly expound on the interest of the state, i.e. what is now defined as 'enlightened national interest'.[6] The goal set before the ruler was to increase relative power and influence through expansion, either territorially or in terms of alliances. Kautilya wanted the ruler to aspire to be a *vijigishu*, one desirous of conquering other territories. The territory referred to could be physical territory, psychological influence and even physical dominance.[7] The *vijigishu's* aim was to ensure *yogakshema* and *lokasangraha* of his subjects. *Yogakshema* means to ensure welfare of the state and subjects implying happiness, prosperity, peace and bliss of his people so as to achieve *lokasangraha* which means, to do what is beneficial to people.[8] Kautilya wanted the ruler to create conditions within the state where adequate opportunity existed for each citizen to practice his potential profession to the best of his capability, in relative abandon, to ensure economic development. This led to the three goals of life namely, *dharma* (righteous and dutiful life), *artha* (economic well-being) and *kama* (enjoyment of pleasures). Amongst these three goals, Kautilya assigned *artha* the foremost place.[9] He stated that both *dharma* and *kama* flourish only when the focus is on the acquisition of *artha.*[10] Kautilya is unique in ancient Indian thought in being both practical and pragmatic. He comes about as one who discards the utopian, impractical, high moral ground for the more utilitarian and sensible mode of thought.

The foremost national interest was to ensure and secure the economic well-being of the state in order to ensure protection and flourishing of its subjects. The Ruler's duty (*rajadharma)* predominantly ensured the security of the individual and society as also protecting and justice. In order to ensure that the subjects adhere to discipline and their assigned duties, *danda* or legitimate coercive authority of the state, is exercised in *rajadharma.* Consequently, the ultimate basis of political society or the state is *danda.*[11] In other words, enlightened and enforced disciplined polity is the basis of an economically viable, strong and prosperous nation. Kautilya proceeded to expound upon the methods of attaining these objectives. He stated that the essence of the entire apparatus of the state in the end is towards happiness.[12] The *Arthashastra* laid down the *modus operandi* for achieving this end state. Kautilya classified *prakritis* or the seven elements of a state,[13] elaborated on *shadgunya*—six methods of foreign policy,[14] delved into different methods of conflict resolution, detailing the five types of wars, another unique feature of Kautilya's *Arthashastra* [15] and finally the crown jewel of this work namely the *Rajamandala* Doctrine.[16]

Prakritis (Elements of the State)

The elements, *prakritis,* which constitute various components of a state are seven in number.[17] These can be termed as capabilities or capacities of a nation. These capabilities enable a nation to derive power by strengthening their innate sub-components. They are:

(a) The Ruler (*swamin*)
(b) The group of ministers and officials (*amatya*),

(c) The territory and population of the state (the *janapada*),
(d) The fortified towns and cities (*durga*)
(e) The treasury (*kosha*)
(f) The military forces (*danda*)
(g) The allies (*mitra*)

Fig. 1: Prakritis: Constituents of National Capabilities/Capacities

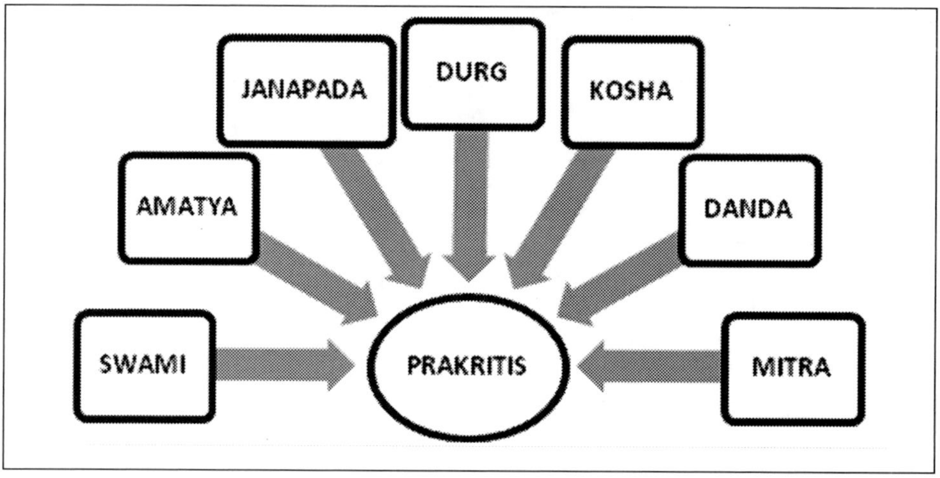

In order to derive a better understanding of the *prakritis,* we could resort to juxtaposing these seven elements (*prakritis*) on the present-day state structures. This would enable us to get a better understanding of the relevance of this exposition. The *swamin* in a democracy would be the political leadership. The *amatya,* undertakes executive and judicial duties, would be the bureaucracy and judiciary. The term *janapada* would refer to the natural resources, demography, territorial boundaries of the state, its traditions, culture, education and training systems, its industrial might and necessary skillsets.

The term *durga* refers to the national infrastructure, the term *kosha* relates to the economic strength and financial architecture of the state while *danda* would be the security forces (both internal and external security). The term *mitra* would imply international alliances with other global states. The figure below shows the Kautilya's elements of national power architecture are relevant even today. These are placed in a clockwise manner in the descending order of priority. In other words, the preceding element is deemed more important than the latter.[18] These connotations would translate into the structure given below:

Fig. 2: Sources of National Power (*Mandala Yonih*) in the *Arthashastra*

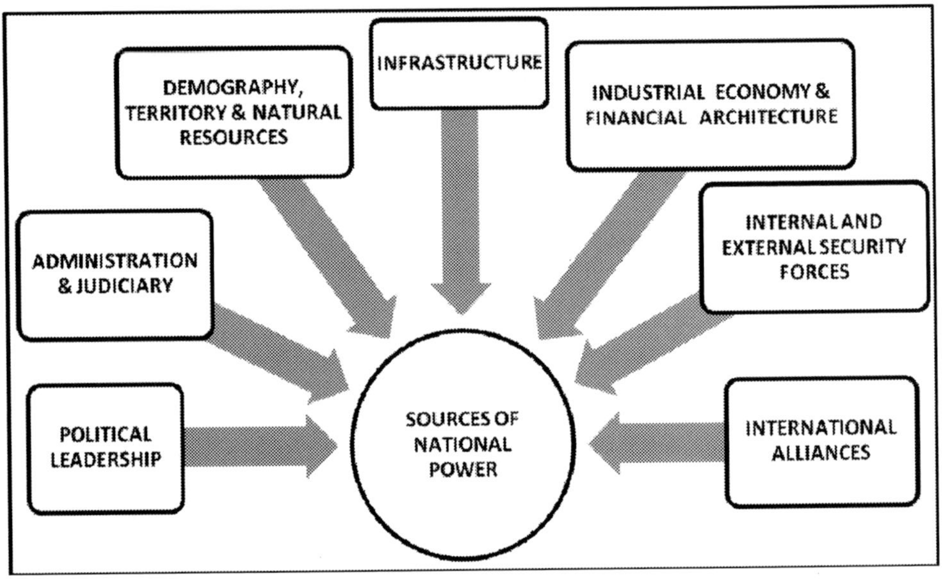

Sources of Power and Accomplishing National Objectives.

The *Arthashastra* states that strength is power and accomplishment of national objectives is the eventual happiness and that these four are interrelated.[19] There are three *shaktis* or powers that operate in a state in the ascending order of importance. *utsahashakti* is the personal energy, focus, grit and drive of both the leadership and state's populace along with the enabling factors. It is termed 'preferential power' as it is an intangible function of intrinsic choice; *prabhushakti*, the power of the economy, enabling infrastructure and the military. It is termed as 'physical power' as it is tangible, extrinsic and can be measured. *Mantrashakti* is the power of knowledge and intellect of the leadership, bureaucracy as well as the populace. This could be termed as 'knowledge and information power.' It is similar to 'soft power' as enunciated by Joseph Nye[20] but is much more encompassing in its domain and is a subject for further discussion.

Before starting any major foreign policy initiative, the *vijigishu* must satisfy himself that he is superior in three respects. Kautilya opines that any endeavour with a foreign nation should compose of smart and comprehensive use of the three powers used singly as well as in combination. Thus, a combination of all three powers could be termed as CNP.

It is the judicious mix of these three powers which will enable a nation to draw out a grand strategy towards accomplishing the national objectives. The above could be tabulated thus:[21]

Table 1: Three Types of Powers in a State

Strength	*Power*
(a) Knowledge, Intellect, Diplomacy, Culture	Intellectual Power (*Mantrashakti*) *(Knowledge and Information Power)*
(b) Economic and Military Strength	Power of Material Resources (*Prabhushakti*) *(Hard Power)*
(c) Courage, Focussed and Spirited Leadership and Populace	Energetic and Spirited Power (*Utsahashakti*) *(Preferential Power)*

Therefore, if the two concepts of *prakritis* and *shaktis* are combined, we would come to a representation of a framework of Comprehensive National Power. The *prakritis* and the three powers could be juxtaposed to the current understanding to glean out a model which could be the basis for a CNP model for any country. It highlights the importance of 'knowledge and information power' over 'economic and military power' (hard power). A Combination of these three powers (Hard, Knowledge and Preferential) would result in the exercise of Comprehensive National Power of a nation. Thus an integrated approach to create a conceptual framework of the Kautilyan model of relating National Capabilities to National Powers could deliver the required thought construct to create a Comprehensive National Power structure.

According to Kautilya, the objectives of a nation's leadership, while securing its own power, should be to continuously lookout to acquire newer sources of power, consolidate them, expand and maximise these sources and lastly to allow the fruits of this increased power percolate down to the masses. Comprehensive National Power model as culled out from the *Arthashastra* is as given in Figure 3.

Fig. 3: Kautilya's CNP in Modern Day Lexicon

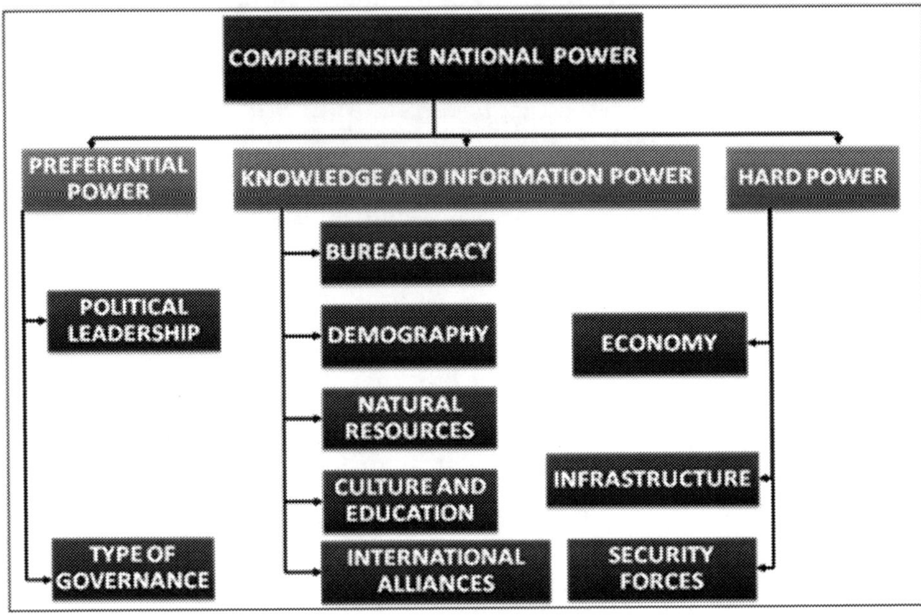

Relative power matrices need to be considered before making any grand strategy with respect to another nation or entity. These unravel the relative balance of power and would then provide sovereign options in selecting the correct course of action. While Knowledge and Information Power lays the foundation of an effective and active foreign policy, however, in order to effectively and completely overpower any adversary, the conqueror would need to focus on beefing up the state CNP. Therefore, a dynamic relationship exists between the national objectives and power, mediated and balanced by the right foreign policy. This, when applied to the neighbourhood states which surround the state, is termed as the *rajamandala siddhanta*, the Doctrine of Circle of Ruling Powers.

Doctrine of *Rajamandala*

Kautilya propounded and developed a unique doctrine of foreign policy, aptly called the *rajamandala* or the *Circle of Ruling Powers*. This doctrine propounds that a country's immediate neighbours could be a hostile adversary, neutral or a vassal state while their neighbours would be natural allies of the said country. In other words, if the said nation-state is in the centre, an immediate concentric circle would be adversarial or neutral, while the next concentric circle of nation-states with contiguous boundaries to the adversaries would be its natural allies. The concentric circles would then be expanded to give the same relationships so on and so forth. To put it plainly, an adversary's adversary is a friend.

The *Arthashastra* states that strength is power and accomplishment of national objectives is the eventual happiness that a state desires and that these four are interrelated.[22] The terms given by Kautilya to the constituents of the *rajamandala* are *vijigishu* (conqueror), *ari* (adversary), *mitra* (ally), *ari-mitra* (adversary's ally), *mitra-mitra* (ally's ally), *parshnigraha* (adversary in the rear), *akranda* (ally in the rear), *madhyama* (Middle Ruler), *udasina* (Neutral Ruler).[23] The Middle Ruler, *madhyama,* is one with territory adjoining both the *vijigishu* and the *ari* and is powerful than either of them. The Neutral Ruler, *udasina*, was one whose borders are farther away but is far more stronger and powerful than the Middle Ruler. Kautilya puts forth the *mandala* theory wherein the *vijigishu, ari, madhyama* and *udasina*, each have a *mandala* (circle of capabilities) which is constituted with 18 components.[24] The *rajamandala* treats each state as a part of a triad (state, state's friend and friend's friend), with four such triads of the *vijigishu, ari, madhyama* and *udasina* forming the *rajamandala*.

Kautilya restricted the number of constituent states in a *mandala* to three after discussing at length a lot of variables. The three state *mandala* was found to be the most stable and conducive to peace and development. Incidentally, this is borne out even by modern-day game theory research.[25] The *vijigishu* needs to plan increasing his relative power in different ways according to the circumstances prevailing with the other three *mandala*s (of the *ari, madhyama and udasina*) at that point of time. The *rajamandala* treats each state as a part of a triad (state, state's friend and friend's friend), with four such triads making up the *mandala* of the *vijigishu, ari, madhyama and udasina*. The central idea being relative power between each of these constituents is the sole determinant for the policy to be used towards cementing long term gains. In order to exploit the doctrine of *rajamandala* effectively, Kautilya propounded six methods of foreign policy called the *shadgunya*. These six methods of foreign policy contribute to increasing

Fig. 4: Constitution of a *Mandala* of the Vijigishu

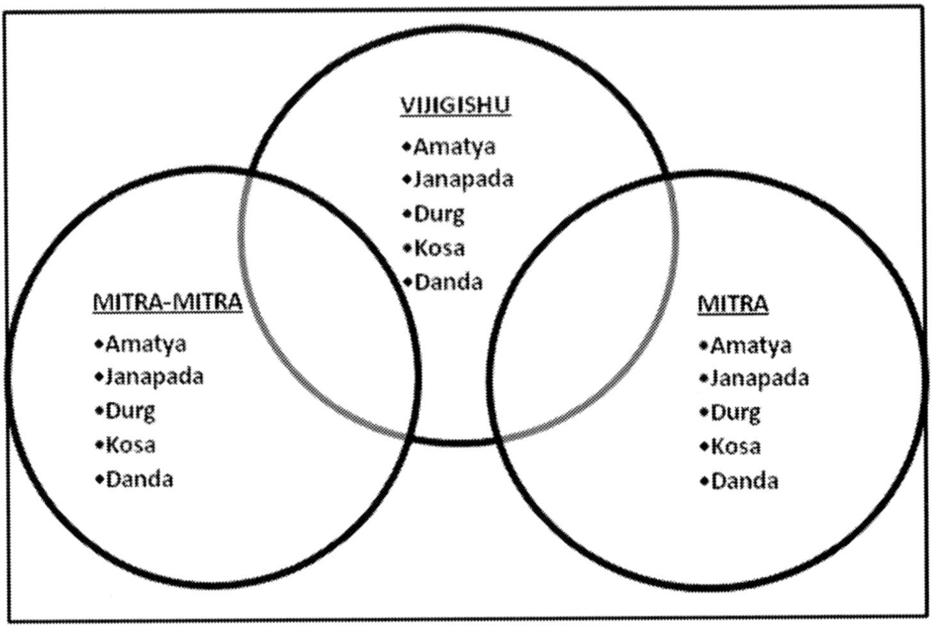

the effective national power of the state.[26] These were not uniquely formulated by Kautilya. These have been in existence since ancient times. These have been a part and parcel of ancient Indian lore and are also elaborated in the *Mahabharata*.[27] However, he elaborates extensively on the various methodologies of utilising them. Moreover, there are four basic conflict resolution methods and three complex advanced methods laid out in the *Arthashastra* which are termed as *upayas*.[28] Exploiting the *shadgunya* combined with a suitable *upaya*, a *vijigishu* can ensure that he achieves his national goals of *yogakshema, lokasangraha* and becoming a *chakravartin* ruler. The purpose of all policies is that the national leadership (*swamin*) increases the CNP while keeping in mind the ethical consequences of any action in the long run.[29]

Regenerative Cycle of Proactive Approach

In order to increase CNP and achieve national objectives, Kautilya propounds the leadership to wage war, i.e. to adopt a proactive approach. However, before adopting a proactive approach, he stresses a lot on the extensive consideration that is given to measure differential or relative power. He classifies the various types of proactive approaches into five different ways[30] which are:

(a) *Prakashayuddha:* Open War[31]
(b) *Kutayuddha:* Deception War[32] (or war by deceit and treachery)
(c) *Tusnimyuddha:* Silent War[33] (in modern days it could be termed as cyberwar)
(d) *Mantrayuddha:* Information War or Psychological War[34]
(e) *Gudhayuddha:* Irregular and Concealed War

These proactive approaches are used only after assessing own *mandala* as well as the *rajamandala*. A proactive approach is initiated to maximise own capabilities (*prakritis*) as compared to that of the adversary. This process needs to be repeated with each *prakriti* till own relative power is maximised in the *rajamandala*. The process of increasing the CNP using this theoretical framework could be termed as the Regenerative Cycle of Proactive Approach.

Fig. 5: Maximising CNP Utilising the Regenerative Cycle of Proactive Approach

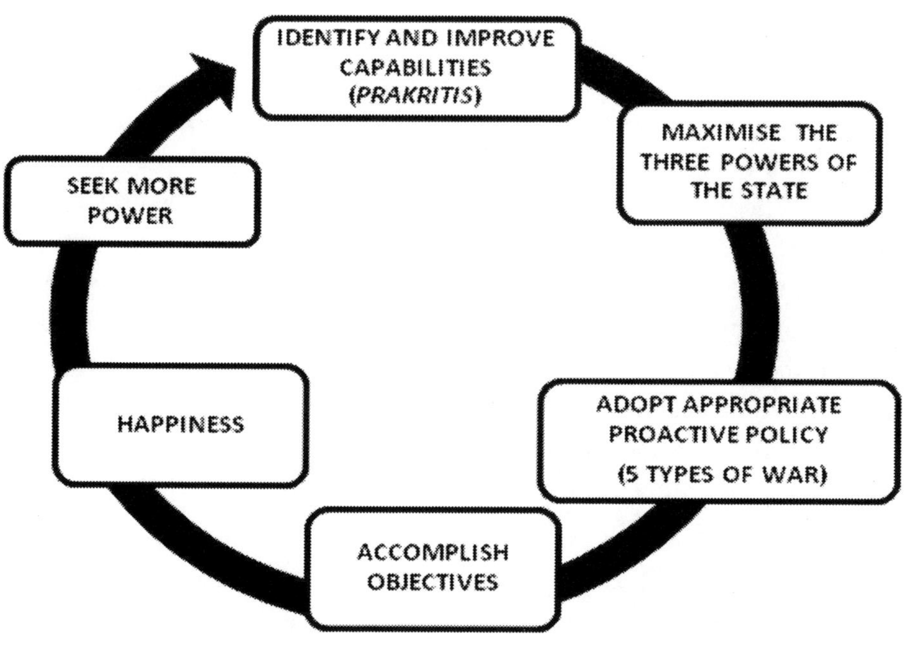

Relevance to Modern International Relations Thought

Comprehensive National Power is the bedrock of inter-state relations. This is the intrinsic assumption of Kautilya's *magnum opus*, the *Arthashastra*. Kautilya's theory of a realist state steeped deep in *realpolitik*, is markedly unique as it bases its realism and the monopoly of violence of the state on ethical values which are in the larger interest of the society, not just focused on the increase in state power. He advocates that the state's political leadership should strive to be in the mould of a *dharmavijayin*. This is in marked contrast to the celebrated Western view of the renowned German scholar, Max Weber's theory of Realism and *Realpolitik*.[35]

All forms of modern realism hold on to three basic assumptions. First, relations among nations are innately and intrinsically conflictual. Secondly, political life is organised around groups, whether they are clans, tribes, *mahajanapadas*, kingdoms or nation-states.[36] Thirdly, human nature strives for power and security.[37] However, as seen in this paper, it is Kautilya who for the first time laid the bedrock of realism on an extensive analysis of state dynamics and behavioural psychology. The three-state *mandala* is another unique pioneering feature of this CNP model which has been borne out to be true even by modern research,[38] though Kautilya has not been given due credit for the same.

Another fallacy is that the Doctrine of *rajamandala* is essentially a Balance of Power equivalent.[39] However, the Doctrine of *rajamandala* is a framework which encompasses three modern theories, namely the Balance of Power Theory, the Hegemony Theory as well as the Power Transition Theory.[40] It attacks the very core belief of Balance of Power theorists "that hegemonies do not form in multistate systems because perceived threats of hegemony over the system generate balancing behavior by other leading states in the system."[41] It advocates the need for the *vijigishu* to become a *chakravartin* (meaning a hegemon) by increasing his CNP in a progressive and calculated manner. Incidentally, there has been, of late, international research questioning the historical validity of the Balance of Power Theory that hegemons do not form.[42]

Warfare is central to the rise and fall of any nation's power. Indeed, it determines the rise of a nation within the relative balance of power of its neighbourhood. In modern times, open war is less preferred and the other types of war, which Kautilya postulated 2300 years back, have now become the choice of sovereign options. Therefore, a calibrated approach focused on increasing the Comprehensive National Power is the way forward in increasing the influence as a nation in the geopolitical scenario. Kautilya laid down the grand strategy of developing a nation from the very nascent stage of its development into a powerful and influential nation. These principles are timeless being the essence of wisdom gleaned from the burden of 5000 years of history which India has stood testimony to. Therefore, any nation aspiring to attain its rightful place in the world polity could follow Kautilya's Regenerative Cycle of Proactive Approach to maximise its Comprehensive National Power.

NOTES

1. "Excerpts of the speech of Prime Minister P.V. Narasimha Rao quoting Kautilya in Beijing University, September 9, 1993", at http://www.ignca.nic.in/ks_41006.htm (Accessed on October 16, 2012).
2. R.P. Kangle, *The Kautiliya Arthasastra Part III*, Bombay University Press, Mumbai, 1965, p. 266.
3. Roger Boesche, "Kautilya's Arthasastra on War and Diplomacy in Ancient India", in *The Journal of Military History*, 67(1), January 2003, p. 10.
4. *Manusyanam vrttir arthah manusyavati bhumirityarthah. Tasyah prithivya labhapalanopayah shastram arthashastram iti.* (In R.P. Kangle, *The Kautiliya Arthasastra Part I*, Motilal Banarsidass, New Delhi, p. 280, [15.1.1-2].
5. R.P. Kangle, note 2, p. 2. The *Arthashastra* contains fifteen *adhikarana*s or Books. Of these, the first five deal with what is called *tantra* or the internal administration of the state while the next eight deal with the *avapa* or its relations with neighbouring states. The last two are miscellaneous in nature.
6. "Excerpts of Prime Minister Dr. Manmohan Singh's talk while addressing the Heads of Missions Conference in New Delhi on December 23", at http://www.indian embassy.org/India_Review/2009/Jan%202009.pdf (Accessed on October 12, 2012). Dr. Manmohan Singh emphasised that India's foreign policy should be an extension of "our enlightened national interests." Incidentally, "enlightened self-interest" was a concept discussed by French Philosopher Alexis de Tocqueville, in his work 'Democracy in America' written in 1840. He described the concept wherein Americans voluntarily came together in associations to further the interests of the group and also thereby, to serve their own interests.
7. R.P. Kangle, *The Kautiliya Arthasastra Part I*, Motilal Banarsidass, New Delhi, 2010, p. 247, [12.1.10-16]. There are three types of *vijigishus* distinguished: *dharmavijayin,* who makes conquests for the sake of glory and is satisfied with mere submission by other kings; *lobhavijayin*, who makes conquests out of greed and is out to obtain

land or money or both; *asuravijayin*, who makes conquests like a demon and seizes land, money, sons and wives of the conquered king and takes the king's life.

8. Hemangini Jai, "Lokasamgraha in Kautilya", in K.P. Jog (ed.), *Perceptions on Kautiliya Arthaśāstra: in Commemoration of Prof. R.P. Kangle Birth Centenary*, Popular Prakashan Pvt. Ltd., Mumbai, 1999.
9. Narasingha Prosad Sil, *Kautilya's Arthaśāstra: a Comparative Study*, Academic Publishers, New Delhi, 1985, pp. 21-22.
10. R.P. Kangle, note 7, p. 8, [1.7.6-7]. *Artha eva pradhana iti Kautilyah. Arthamulau hi dharmakamaviti.*
11. *Ibid.*, p. 23.
12. *Ibid.,* p. 166, [6.2.32].
13. R.P. Kangle, *The Kautiliya Arthasastra Part II*, Bombay University Press, Mumbai, 1972, p. 314.
14. Ibid., pp. 512-514.
15. R.P. Kangle, note 2, pp. 258-259.
16. *Ibid.,* pp. 248-251.
17. L.N. Rangarajan, *Kautilya: The Arthashastra*, Penguin Books, New Delhi, 2000, p. 97.
18. R.P. Kangle, note 7, pp. 385-390. In case any *vyasana* (calamity or adversity) befalls on *prakritis* equally, that which could cause more damage should be considered serious and attended to. Thus the order or priority would be the political leadership followed by the bureaucracy, territory and population, infrastructure and industry, economy, military and international alliances.
19. R.P. Kangle, *ibid.*, p. 166, [6.2.31-32]. The sutras 6.2.31-32 are "Balam Shaktih II Sukham Siddhih II" meaning "Power is Strength. The accomplishment of objectives leads to happiness." This is the central idea of Kautilya's *Arthashastra* and he expounds on this critical area throughout the next seven chapters.
20. Joseph S. Nye, Jr., "Soft Power", in *Foreign Policy*, No. 80, Twentieth Anniversary, Autumn 1990, p. 166, at http://www.foreignpolicy.com/Ning/archive/archive/080/SOFT_POWER.PDF (Accessed on October 14, 2012).
21. L.N. Rangarajan, note 17, pp. 525-526.
22. R.P. Kangle, note 7.
23. *Ibid.,* pp. 517-523.
24. In addition to the *swamin* (leadership), the constituents of the *mandala* include the *amatya, janapada, durga, kosha, danda* of each of the three member states of the *mandala.*
25. R. Harrison Wagner, "The Theory of Games and the Balance of Power", in *World Politics*, 38(4), July 1986, pp. 546-576. Wagner utilises game theory to investigate several controversial issues in the literature on the balance of power. A simple model of an international system is presented as an n-person non-cooperative game in extensive form, and the stability of both constant-sum and non-constant sum systems are examined. It is shown not only those constant-sum systems with any number of actors from two to five can be stable, but also that stability is actually promoted by conflict of interests. Contrary to much of the literature, however, there is a well-defined sense in which the most stable system is one with three actors. In each type

of system, there is at least one distribution of power that leads not only to system stability but also to peace. Some of these peaceful distributions are more stable than others, and these more stable distributions are shown to be characterised by inequality rather than by equality of power. It is possible to distinguish between a bipolar and a multi-polar type of stable distribution, the properties of each of which resemble, to some degree, assertions made about them in the literature.

26. L.N. Rangarajan, note 17, p. 512.
27. *Vidura Niti*, verse 43. English Translation by K.M. Ganguli, at http://hinduholypdfbooks.blogspot.in/2014/07/vidura-niti-sanskrit-text-with-english.html

    एकया द्वे विनिश्चित्य त्रींश्चतुर्भिर्वशे कुरु ।

    पञ्च जित्वा विदित्वा षट्सप्त हित्वा सुखी भव ॥ ४३ ॥

    Discriminating the two (what is to be done and what is not to be done) by means of the one (the intellect), bringing under thy subjection the three (friend, enemy and the neutral person) by means of four (the four means of success against an enemy—*sama*, reconciliation or negotiation; *dana*, bribery; *bheda*, sowing dissensions; and *danda*, punishment), and also conquering the five (senses of perception) and knowing the six (six expedients to be used in foreign politics—*sandhi*, *vigraha*, *yana*, *asana*, *dvaidhibhava* and *samshraya*) and abstaining from the seven (woman, gambling, hunting, intoxicants, harsh speech, harsh punishment and amassing wealth using unjust means), be happy.
28. R.P. Kangle, note 13, p. 133, 425, [2.18.19, 9.6.56-62]. *Upayas*: These are *sama*—adopting a conciliatory attitude, *dana*—placating with rewards and gifts, *bheda*—sowing dissension amongst enemies and *danda*—using force. The three advanced methods are *upeksha*—stepping back, ignoring deliberately, being indifferent; *maya*—passive deception and *aindrajala*—active deception. The recommended methods in case of next of kin are *sama, dana or upeksha*. In case of placating the military, people in the countryside or citizens of the city *dana, bheda and maya* are the right methods. In case of a neighbouring prince or forest chiefs, use of *bheda, danda and aindrajala* is recommended. This order is *anuloma* (natural order of progression of conflict resolution techniques). If the methods are used in the reverse order, it is called *pratiloma.* However, Kautilya encourages use of the simple conflict resolution methods initially before adopting the use of complex resolution methods.
29. R.P. Kangle, note 2, p. 251.
30. This was in variance to the accepted two types of *dharmayuddha* and *kutayuddha.*
31. R.P. Kangle, note 7, p. 178 [7.6.17].
32. *Ibid.*
33. *Ibid.*
34. *Ibid.,* p. 247, [12.1.17].
35. John M. Hobson and Leonard Seabrooke, "Reimagining Weber: Constructing International Society and the Social Balance of Power", in *European Journal of International Relations*, 7(2), June 2001, pp. 257-60.
36. H.J. Morgenthau, *Politics among Nations: The Struggle for Power and Peace*, Alfred A. Knopf., New York, 1948, pp. 4-15.

37. R. Gilpin, "The Richness of the Tradition of Political Realism", in R.O. Keohane (ed.), *Neorealism and Its Critics*, Columbia University Press, New York, 1986, pp. 301-21.
38. Emerson M.S. Niou and Peter C. Ordeshook, "A Theory of the Balance of Power in International Systems", in *Journal of Conflict Resolution*, 30(4), December 1986, pp. 698-701.
39. Brian Healy and Arthur Stein, "The Balance of Power in International History: Theory and Reality", in *Journal of Conflict Resolution*, 17(1), March 1973, pp. 33-61.
40. A.F.K. Organski and Jacek Kugler, *The War Ledger*, University of Chicago Press, Chicago, 1980. Power Transition Theory argues that when the dominant state in the international system is overtaken in internal power capabililities by a dissatisfied challenger, the likelihood of conflict increases significantly. The *Arthashastra* adds to the missing notion to the Power Transition Theory construct by taking into account the external power additions too, by way of the *mandala*.
41. Jack S. Levy, "What do Great Powers Balance Against and When?", in T.V. Paul, James J. Wirtz and Michel Fortmann (eds.), *Balance of Power: Theory and Practice in the 21st Century*, Stanford University Press, Stanford, 2004, pp. 36-38.
42. William C. Wohlforth et al., "Testing Balance-of-Power Theory in World History", in *European Journal of International Relations*, 13(2), 2007, pp. 155-185.

5

Varieties of *Mitras* and Varieties of *Sandhis* in Early India: Kautilya's *Arthashastra* and other Texts*

Krishnendu Ray

Prelude

Human beings take measures in different ways to defend their existence on the earth. Historically we come to know that they have chosen and lived in a territory under the chief as they needed protection and social regulation.[1] The chief/king (*raja*) was mainly a military leader who defended the settlement.[2] Eventually, we come to the kingdom of the king. He consolidated his power and authority. Historically, we know the establishment of kingdoms under the king (*raja*). In this connection, we may refer to the emergence of territorial kingdoms textually recorded as *mahajanapadas*. These *mahajanapadas* were mostly situated in north India. These were such as Kashi (the area adjoining Varanasi, Uttar Pradesh), Kosala (Lucknow, Gonda, Faizabad and Baharaich districts of Uttar Pradesh), Anga (Bhagalpur, Bihar), Magadha (southern Bihar), Vrji (modern Basadh, northern Bihar), Cedi (the area around Jabalpur, Madhya Pradesh),

*For this paper I remain grateful to my teacher Prof. Ranabir Chakravarti, JNU, New Delhi.

Vatsa (near Allahabad, Uttar Pradesh), Matsa (located in eastern Rajasthan), Surasena (Mathura, Uttar Pradesh), Avanti (Ujjain and Mahishmati in western Madhya Pradesh), etc.[3] Now, a *mahajanapada* (larger than a *janapada*) emerged when its king absorbed the territory of another *janapada* (territory inhabited by people under the rule of a king) and therefore the creation of a *mahajanapada* was associated with the king's attitude of expansion.[4] This leads one to think that these *mahajanapadas* emerged by annexing other contemporary lesser powers in north India. Gradually, Kosala, Vatsa, Avanti and Magadha became the four most prominent monarchical *mahajanapadas*,[5] naturally, the question of providing protection to the people of the kingdom became an issue. Consequently, the king had to take measures in order to resist the evil influences of the enemy. Therefore, the king resorted to war (*yuddha*). Magadha emerged as the victorious power by around 300 BCE.[6]

In this connection, we can refer to the measure of Bimbisara (c. 545/44-493 BCE) of the Haryanka Dynasty of Magadha. He followed the diplomatic policy of marriage alliances with the ruling families of Madra, Kosala and Vaishali. Thus, he accepted these powers as his allies (*mitra*). His political position seems to have been strengthened. Bimbisara territorially annexed his enemy (*ari*) kingdom of Anga to his expanding kingdom.[7] In this task his friendship with those powers might have been helpful. He did not want to alienate any military chief of the time. The Haryanka ruler is also known to have obliged his Gandharian friend by receiving the latter's embassy. Side by side, Bimbisara is also said to have medically helped Pradyota, the king of Avanti, by providing the latter with physician Jivaka.[8] Thus, Bimbisara paved his way for having friendship from his contemporary counterparts. It, therefore, appears that the king requires the ally for the strength of his political position. It appears that the Magadhan king occupied other territorial kingdoms, acquired wealth, possessed Pataliputra which was commercially important and strategically better located than Rajagriha.[9] The Magadhan king must have capably and efficiently utilised all these possessions and thus taken Magadha to the most powerful political position in early India. In doing so, actually the Magadhan king had to tackle his other contestants in different ways. However, the ally is a constituent element of the kingdom. Besides, the other constituent elements that the kingdom requires to possess in order to secure its political existence are such as the king (*svami*), the minister (*amatya*) the country (*janapada*), the fortified city (*durga*), the treasury (*kosha*) and the army (*danda*). We are told *amatyasampat, janapadasampat, mitrasampat*, etc. Thus, we come to the *Arthashastra* of Kautilya (c. 3rd century BCE to c. 1st century CE).[10] According to the text, these are the seven constituent elements of the kingdom.[11] The *Kautiliya Arthashastra* points out how the king can acquire (*labha*) territory and how he should protect (*palana*) his territory. These two things involve the conquest of territory and the framing of policy of the kingdom.[12]

Scholars on the *Kautiliya Arthashastra*

The *Kautiliya Arthashastra* has received scholarly attention. Roger Boesche has studied the *Kautiliya Arthashastra* in connection with his understanding of war and diplomacy in ancient India. In doing so, he has dished out references to the ally and the treaty.[13] Similarly, Chandrasekaran Pravin has also discussed Kautilya's politics, ethics and statecraft and mentioned the friend and the treaty.[14] V.R. Ramachandra Dikshitar has mentioned the list of a few types of *sandhis* (treaties) in connection with the six-fold policy (*sadgunyam*) and the allies of the circle of kings (*mandalayoni*) in his discussion on war in ancient India.[15] S.L. Roy in the context of his discussion on diplomacy in ancient India has discussed the laws of peace and the inter-statal relations in which he has referred to the friend and the treaty.[16] Recently, Patrick Olivelle has discussed the semantics of the two technical terms *samdhi* and *vigraha* discussing Kangle's translation of the same as 'war and peace'.[17] Thus a few scholarly studies relating to the *Kautiliya Arthashastra* are mentioned here. The present study is therefore confined particularly to the varieties of allies and varieties of treaties as known from the the *Kautiliya Arthashastra* and other textual records. However, territorial kingdoms had come into existence by the period when the *Kautiliya Arthashastra* was composed and the prime duties of the rulers of kingdoms were to provide protection to the subjects and to ensure their development and progress. For this the king might have required the ally as well as the alliance with another power in order to iron out the impediments on the way to the goal.

Mandalayoni, Sadgunas and *Upayas:* Background Study of *Mitra* and *Sandhi*

It appears from the *mahajanapada* phase in early Indian history that the king with intellect, strength, and farsightedness, etc. [cf. *atmasampada* (excellences) of the king][18] became successful in the territorial advancement of his power and authority. For this he strengthened his political position not only with his own elements, but also required those of the other king whom the former thought his ally. For, the king had also to face enmity or opposition from other kings. So, the search for the ally led to the inter-state relationship. Thus, we come close to Kautilya's well known circle of kings (*mandalayoni*). The circle of kings points out the location of both the enemy and the ally *vis-a-vis* the conquering king. The king immediately next to the *vijigisu* (conquering) king is the constituent called enemy (*bhumyantara ariprakriti*); if the king with his territory is separated by another territory, he is called the ally of the *vijigisu* king (*bhumyekantara mitraprakritih*). Thus, in front of the conqueror lie the ally (*mitra*), the enemy's ally (*arimitra*), the ally's ally (*mitramitra*), and then the enemy's ally's ally (*arimitramitra*). Kautilya is well aware that the conquering king may be attacked by the enemy from the rear also. Therefore the kings lying behind the conquering king are considered as *parsnigraha* (rear enemy), *akranda* (rear friend called for), *parsnigrahasara* (friend of the rear enemy), *akrandasara* (friend of the rear friend).[19] Along with these we come across another two terms *madhyama* (middle king) and *udasina* (neutral king) in Kautilya's *mandalayoni*. Kautilya informs that the king whose kingdom is contiguous to those of the conquering king and the enemy king, capable of helping or of suppressing them when they are united or separated, is called *madhyama*. The king whose kingdom with its constituent elements is beyond the sphere of those of the conquering king, the enemy and the *madhyama*, who is stronger than them in terms of their constituents and capable of assisting them when they are united or separated (*samhatasamhatanam*) and of suppressing them when they are in hostility, is known as the *udasina*.[20] So, the *udasina* appears to have been very powerful among the three powers—the enemy (*ari*), the conqueror (*vijigisu*) and the middle king (*madhyama*). Therefore, we notice the two characteristics of *madhyama* and *udasina* and these are their location and strength. The *madhyama* is a potential enemy to the *vijigisu* as it is coterminous to both the conquering king and his enemy. Therefore Kautilya asks the conquering king to conquer the territory of his immediate enemy and then that of the *madhyama*, after that, the kingdom of *udasina*.[21] It therefore appears that the king is intent upon establishing his lordship over other rulers of the circle. Such a king has been described as *chakravartin*.[22] In other words, for the king it was a process of attaining the status of the *chakravartin* ruler who was superior to the rulers of other kingdoms. The result was constant warfare. In this circumstance it was hardly possible for a king to remain isolated. This led him to find out an ally. We may remember that Magadha brought both Kosala and Vrji under it. Thus Magadha became a dominating power in eastern India. Then Magadha eclipsed Avanti which enjoyed the superior political position in western India.

However, it may be difficult for any power to remain truly neutral in the midst of contending powers.[23] We may note that the *udasina* may remain as a neutral[24] power so long its interests are unaffected.[25] The existence of *udasina* and *madhyama* within the circle of kings was thought to be necessary for considering the line of action to be adopted in a conflict between a particular kingdom and its enemy. These two powers were probably to take sides in the conflict. However, in every conflict the *udasina* and the *madhyama* were not necessarily drawn, according to N.N. Law.[26] In the absence of the *udasina* and the *madhyama,* the conquering king by his superior policy, according to Kautilya, should overcome the enemy.[27] In this connection in the *Mahabharata*, we find that the king was asked to be aware (*budhyethah*) of his own position as well as that of his enemy of the circle (*mandalani—paresam-atmanastatha*) and also of the activities of both *udasina* and *madhyama*.[28] The king who for his life and wealth takes shelter from the conquering king is known as the ally made. The king who is related through the mother or father is known as the ally by birth.[29] The *Mahabharata* also refers to the natural (*sahaja*) friend.[30] At this point, historically, we may remember that the Gupta ruler Chandragupta II's (376/7-414 CE)[31] daughter Prabhavatigupta was given in marriage to Rudrasena II of the most powerful Vakataka ruling house of central India. Her youngest son Pravarasena II (420-452 CE)[32] through his mother was related to the Guptas. Chandragupta II also established matrimonial alliance with the

Nagas, an important northern Malwa power in north Indian politics,[33] by marrying the Naga princess Kuveranaga and thus he befriended them. The purpose was probably to secure their support and service to the Gupta kingdom and its army. Such marriage alliances might have strengthened the political position of the Gupta ruler. This might have enabled him to destroy the Saka rule in western India as the Gupta king had such an aim to realise it.[34] Similarly, the king who is territorially immediately proximate to the conquering king, equal to the latter by birth, is called the natural enemy, the enemy by birth.[35] The king who is opposed to the conqueror or causes opposition (by someone else) for the conqueror is called the enemy made.[36] In this connection we may propose an epigraphic evidence of the Guptas. According to the Bhitari Stone Pillar Inscription of Skandagupta (456-467 CE), one militarily and economically developed (*samudita-bala-koshan*) enemy (*amitra*) power (may be Pusyamitras, though it is difficult to ascertain their identity) understandably brought about some troubles for the Gupta emperor Skandagupta. Thus, the former came up with opposition/ trouble which the Gupta emperor successfully vanquished by means of a battle.[37]

However, the goal of the king is to ensure the security and progress of his kingdom putting an end to enmity of any kind. For the successful realisation of the goal, the king therefore requires a proper coordination among three *shaktis* (powers), six *gunas* (*sandhi, vigraha*, etc. measures) and four *upayas* (political expedients *sama, dana, bheda, danda*).[38] Kautilya advises the conquering king that he is to apply six measures of policy according to his power.[39] The powers are of three kinds such as the king's power of intelligence and of knowledge about sciences (*jnabalam mantrashakti*); that of his material resources, particularly the treasury and the army (*koshadandabalam prabhu shakti*); that of his energy, bravery (*vikramabalam utsahashakti*).[40] In connection with the strength of the king we learn that according to Kautilya, the king possessing the strength of material riches and the military force (*prabhu shakti / prabhavashakti)* is superior to the king having the strength of prowess (*utsahashakti*). For, the materially rich king can hire or purchase heroic men. He can bring under his control another king possessing the strength of prowess. Thus, he can overreach the energetic, brave king. However, Kautilya opines that *mantrashakti* is superior. For, the king having the power of knowledge and wisdom can intelligently tackle the situation by the application of four means (*upayas*) like conciliation (*sama*), etc. Thereby, he can overreach the king possessing energy and or material resources.[41]

In the *Mahabharata* also we find that the king is advised to think, before launching an attack against the opponent, whether he is powerful in terms of *mantrashakti*, *prabhushakti*, and *utsahashakti*.[42] It appears that the king is directed to attain power and success or to deny the same to his enemy kingdom.[43] This requires the king to frame and follow the six-fold policy described as *sadgunyam*[44] in the *Arthashastra*. The king is asked to consider which measure in his relation with the other kingdom will suit his purpose best and accordingly he should take that position.[45] At the time of maintaining a particular relation with the other king, the king is also directed to seek advancement which may be accomplished by following one of the four political expedients such as *sama* (conciliation), *dana* (gifts), *bheda* (dissension) and *danda* (force) in diplomatic practices.[46] In the *Mahabharata* also, the king is asked to adopt one or the other of the four political expedients in his favour.[47] However, the six-fold policy consists of *sandhi* (treaty), *vigraha* (*apakaro vigrahah*, initiation of hostile activities/ political strategy without waging a war actually[48]), *asana* (showing indifferent attitude/staying quiet/*upeksanam*), *yana* (marching for augmenting power in terms of ability, time and space), *samshraya* (submitting to the other king for shelter *pararpanam*) and *dvaidhibhava* (dual policy, peace with one, hostility with another). It is said that the six measures are really because of differences in the circumstances.[49] In the *Mahabharata*, the king is advised to think carefully about the application of the six-fold strategy as and when the situation demands.[50] In connection with the six-fold strategy, we find that Kautilya has referred to the views of his earlier authorities (*ityacharyah*) and then his own opinion on the six measures of policy.[51] Thus, we come close to *mitra* and *sandhi*.

Mitra and *Sandhi*: Their Varieties

The term *sandhi*, according to Kautilya, signifies a treaty/alliance between the two kings on conditions of the surrender of land, treasury and army, etc. (*panabandhah sandhih*) or 'a negotiated agreement'.[52] He always prefers peace to war if there is equal advancement in peace or war; for war causes losses, expenses, hindrances, etc.[53] The king is advised to make peace instead of going to war. Therefore, he has attached great importance to the making of an alliance between two or more kings. The author has discussed it under three broad types with twelve subtypes in the *samshrayavritti* section of his *Arthashastra*.[54] The three broad types of *sandhi* are such as *dandaponata sandhi* meaning making *sandhi* by surrendering the army; *koshapanata sandhi* in which the treasury is surrendered and thereby peace is sought and *deshopanata sandhi* (the surrender of land).[55] The *dandaponata sandhi* included three subtypes such as *atmamisha* (waiting upon the enemy with troops), *atmarakshana* (the king saving himself, where the condition is that the commander-in-chief or the crown prince is to wait upon the enemy), and *adristapurusha* (the agreement is that the king himself or the army to go to somewhere else). And the *koshapanata sandhi* consisted of *parikraya* [offering the treasury the other elements of kingdom (*rajya*) are kept free], *upagraha* (the amount to be delivered in instalments), *atyaya* (specifying the time and place for the amount to be paid in each instalment), *kapala* (the whole amount of money to be paid fully at a time) and *suvarna sandhi* ["Tolerable because of payment of a bearable amount in future, even because of a marriage alliance, it would be the 'golden treaty', bringing about union through (mutual) confidence"].[56] However, in connection with the *koshapanata sandhi*, Kautilya informs us about the steps to be taken by the weak king against the stronger king. In that connection, the author mentions some safeguards. Thus, in the first two sub-types of the *koshapanata sandhi*, that is, *parikraya* and *upagraha* the king is advised to deliver forest produce or horses and elephants that have been poisoned. In the third sub-type, that is *atyaya*, the king is directed to pay half of the amount and excuse decline of his all undertakings and therefore decline in his income. In the fourth sub-type, that is *kapala*, the king should defer the payment 'by dilly-dallying and taking time'.[57] In connection with the *deshopanata sandhi* we may remember a historical case. We know that a treaty was signed between Chandragupta Maurya (c. 324-300 BCE) and Seleucus '*Nicator*' putting an end to hostilities between them. According to that treaty, Seleucus ceded Arachosia (Kandahar), Gedrosia (Baluchistan) and Paropomisadai (south-east of Hindu Kush) to Chandragupta Maurya.[58]

However, the *deshopanata sandhi* included four sub-types such as *adista* ('directed' treaty trying to create troubles in the territory surrendered), *ucchinna* ('exterminated' treaty meaning the surrender of the tract wherefrom all wealth have been taken away), *avakraya* ('hire' treaty saving the land by surrendering the produce) and *paradushana* ('ruinous' treaty surrendering the produce completely from lands).[59] However, as regards the *dandaponata sandhi*, *koshapanata sandhi* and *deshopanata sandhi* together we may mention a historical example. We learn from an epigraphic record (dated 770 CE) of the crown-prince (*yuvaraja*) Govinda II of the Rashtrakuta family that Vengi (north of Masulipatnam) was invaded by an army and "the lord of Vengi was humbled by the cession of his treasury, his army and his own country."[60] At this point, we read in the *Mahabharata* that if one king himself is stronger than his opponent, then the stronger king should make an alliance with the opponent bringing in his own favour the fertile land, the skilled army and the experienced minister from the latter.[61]

Now, we are drawn to the making of a treaty with stipulations or without stipulations. Kautilya from that point of view also has drawn our attention to the two varieties of *sandhi*. These are *paripanita sandhi* (treaty with stipulations) with three sub-types such as *paripanitadesha-sandhi* (as to place), *pripanitakala-sandhi* (as to time) and *paripanitartha-sandhi* (as to work) and *aparipanita-sandhi* (treaty without stipulations and without specifying place, time and work; striking at the enemy finding his weak point).[62] In respect of *paripanita-sandhi* both sides enter into a treaty with stipulations as to place, time and objectives to be achieved.[63] In other words, a *sandhi* was aimed at achieving some specific objective(s).[64]

Now, we learn from the *Arthashastra* that if the enemy and the conquering king each want to give help to their respective allies, then the allies who are gainful in turn to the former are fit for the help. From this point of view, Kautilya has drawn our attention to five kinds of allies. They are *shakyarambhi* (capable of accomplishing a work started), *kalyarambhi* (undertaking a work free of defects), *bhavyarambhi* (undertaking a work leading to good results), *sthirakarma* (remaining resolute till the completion of the work undertaken) and *anuraktaprakrti* (one with helpmates accomplishes a work with a little help).[65] It appears that the king has to undertake certain works which are politically, economically and militarily important for the interests of the kingdom. For this, he requires pacts not only for the ally, but also for lands, forests, mines, etc. for ensuring the development of the kingdom.[66] In this connection, Kautilya provides valuable information. The author has referred to *mitrasandhi* (pact for acquiring an ally), *hiranyasandhi* (pact for acquiring money), *bhumisandhi* (pact for acquiring land), *anavasitasandhi* (indetermining pact for a particular work) and *karmasandhi* (construction of forts, etc.).[67] Thus, it appears that the relations between kingdoms in terms of ally, money and land are important. Kautilya maintains that ally, money and land can be kept in a preferential order, the ally and the land being the first and the last in the sequence. In other words money is better than an ally and land is better than money; because it may be possible to gain both an ally and money from gaining a land. And it is also possible to gain an ally from the gain of money.[68] In this connection, our attention is drawn to a good and potential ally. A good ally is one who is permanent and not submissive; one who possesses strength instead of quickness of action; one who possesses the capacity for helping with men instead of money and with money, instead of land. The good ally is one who is constant, renders a small help, but gives it continuously, renders great help for a long time. But the ally who is inconstant, having the capacity to render great help, but deserts for fear of giving help, strives to take back a lot after giving his help.[69] However, Kautilya maintains that acquiring a land ensures the acquisition of the ally and money and therefore the ally who gives the help of land is preferable.[70] Therefore, a perfect ally is said to have such qualities as constant, under control, quickly mobilising, hereditary, great and not double-dealing.[71] In this connection, we find a number of varieties of *mitras* and they are such as *sarvabhoga mitra* (one helping the king with army, land, and money), *chitrabhoga mitra* (one helping with various resources), *mahabhoga mitra* (one greatly helping only with army and money).[72] Therefore, the acquisition of an ally is associated with the fulfilment of certain interests for the kingdom.

Now, in connection with *bhumisandhi*, Kautilya maintains that acquiring a land with permanent enemies ensures the acquisition of more enemies. The land whose frontier areas are not devoid of thieves, the *mlecchhas* and *atavikas* is the land with permanent enemies (*nityamitra*).[73] A permanent enemy remains an enemy, never deserts enmity, even if he is helped or injured. But an impermanent enemy ceases if he is obliged by desisting him from injury. In respect of the acquisition of land we are told that the land that is near, though small (*alpa pratyasanna*), is preferable; because it is easy to obtain, to protect or to get shelter there. But it is not the case with the land which is distant. In this connection the land that is held/defended (*dharyate*) by the army and treasury produced within itself (*svasamutthabhyam koshadandabhyam*) is preferable. But this is not the case with the land that requires the station of the army there for its defence.[74]

However, according to Kautilya, the king is the most important and 'never-exhausted centre of power'. The brief exposition of all other constituent elements of the kingdom is the king and so he is identified with the kingdom (*raja rajyamiti prakritisankshepah*).[75]

Other Texts on *Mitra* and *Sandhi*

This we find changed when we come to authorities like Manu and Yajnavalkya who have described the seven elements of the state (*saptaprakrti*) as seven limbs (*saptanga*).[76] Manu maintains that each one of the seven limbs has a specific task to perform and the limb that can do it is considered as the best for the existence of the kingdom.[77] In the *Mahabharata* also, we find that of the seven limbs (*saptangasya*) the limb that is capable of performing a particular task (*yena yat sidhyate karyam*) assumes importance (*tatpradhanyaya kalpate*).[78] Each of the seven limbs, according to the *Kamandakiya Nitisara*, is complementary to all other limbs for the existence of the kingdom.[79]

We find that the circle of kings, six-fold policy and four political expedients are also supported by another contemporary text called *Yajnavalkyasmriti* (early Christian era). In the text, it is said that the kings in the neighbourhood are called enemies, the kings who reside beyond them are called friends and then the kings unconcerned.[80] The king is asked to keep going on the wheels of the progress of his kingdom keeping the enemy at bay. For its realisation, he is advised to win other kings over to him.

This requires him to apply the four political expedients according to time and circumstances. Thus, its proper application leads to success.[81] We find the Kautiliyan six policies being supported also by the *Yajnavalkyasmriti*.[82] Our attention is drawn to the three results of the treaty such as the ally, gold and land.[83] According to Manu, the king does not prosper by acquiring land and gold so much as by securing a firm (*mitram dhruvam*) ally; however, the ally 'may be of depleted resources at the time', he 'would be powerful in future'.[84] The author asks the king to abandon even the fertile and crop-yielding, safe land for his own well-being.[85] However, according to the *Kamandakiya Nitisara* (c. between 700-750 CE), along with the minister, the fortified city, the treasury and the army, an ally also is a constituent element of the kingdom.[86] The *Kamandakiya Nitisara* has drawn our attention to four kinds of allies such as the ally by birth, the ally by relationship, the ally by heredity and the ally by saving the one from calamities.[87] As Kautilya has treated *sandhi*, so the *Kamandakiya Nitisara* has also mentioned sixteen types of alliances. These are such as *Kapala* (between two powers of equal resources), *upahara* (offering gifts like land or cash or other things), *santana* (establishing relationship through marriage), *samgata* (amity), *upanyasa* (between the two kings intent upon achieving a purpose), *pratikara* (my benefit in return of beneficient services rendered by me), *samyoga* (two parties securing an identical objective), *purusantara, adrstanara, adista, atmamisha, upagraha, parikraya, ucchinna, paribhushana or paradushana,* and *skandhapaneya*.[88] Out of these sixteen types of pacts *upahara* (offering gifts), *parikraya* (surrendering a part of wealth), *ucchinna* (surrendering fertile lands), *paradushana* (surrendering total land produce), *skandhapaneya* (surrendering land product by instalments) emphasise the acquisition of gains from the surrender of wealth. The author attaches importance to the alliance ensuring peace with gifts.[89] According to the author, *upahara* is the only recognised form of *sandhi;* the rest, except *samgata sandhi*, are varieties of the *upahara sandhi (upaharasya bhedah)*.[90] We learn from *Kamandaki* that the king possessing the three powers (*trishaktiyukto*) viz., *mantrashakti, prabhushakti* and *utsahashakti* becomes victorious.[91] However, in the *Agnipurana, mantrashakti* has been considered fitter in comparison to *prabhavashakti* and *utsahashakti* for achieving conquest.[92] For this, the ally was also recognised as one of the seven limbs of the kingdom in the

Agnipurana.[93] We learn from the text that the king should destroy those who obstruct the seven limbs of the kingdom and thereby make efforts for the development (*vriddhi*) of all the circles.[94] Therefore, the king was also asked to be careful about the circle of kings as well as the making of an alliance in connection with his kingdom.[95] However, it is interesting to note that Somadeva also followed up the concepts of the *Arthashastra* tradition comprising *mandala*, *sadgunyam*, and four *upayas* in his *Nitivakyamrita* (the nectar of the *Niti*—lessons). The author has also attached importance to the acquisition of land which, according to him, is better than that of money which is better than acquiring the ally. He has also referred to the importance of the king's three powers (*shaktis*) after Kautilya such as the intellectual, the material and the volitional. According to the author, the strong and superior king should march against the enemy. The weak king is asked to take refuge. The king who loses his strength should make 'peace with agreement', if 'there is no risk of violation of terms'. Thus, U.N. Ghoshal has drawn our attention to the fact that Hemachandra in his *Laghv-Arhannitishastra* (literature on polity) has followed the Kautiliyan tradition in respect of determining the relations between kingdoms. According to the author, the king should make peace when it is likely to yield 'prospective advantage'.[96]

Conclusion

It appears from the above discussion that the king's essential objective is to ensure the security and prosperity of his kingdom. This requires the acquisition of wealth. The ultimate goal of the king is to lead the people of his kingdom in a better way. The king is to go ahead to realise the goal 'actually outmanoeuvring, outwitting, outsmarting the other'.[97] We learn from the *Mahabharata* that no one is a friend or enemy of anyone else.[98]

NOTES

1. Romila Thapar, *Early India from the Origins to AD 1300*, Penguin Books, New Delhi, 2003, p. 119.
2. *Ibid.*, p. 120.
3. Ranabir Chakravarti, *Exploring Early India up to c. AD 1300,* Macmillan Publishers, New Delhi, 2013, pp. 80-81.

4. *Ibid.*, p. 79; Ranabir Chakravarti, *Warfare for Wealth Early Indian Perspective*, Firma KLM Private Ltd., Calcutta, 1986, p. 28.
5. Ranabir Chakravarti, *Warfare for Wealth Early Indian Perspective*, Firma KLM Private Ltd., Calcutta, 1986, pp. 81-82.
6. *Ibid.*, pp. 26-60; Ranabir Chakravarti, note 3, p. 89.
7. *Ibid.*, p. 84. H.C. Raychaudhuri, *Political History of Ancient India Commentary by B.N. Mukherjee*, Oxford University Press, Delhi, 1996, p.182.
8. H.C. Raychaudhuri, *Political History of Ancient India Commentary by B. N. Mukherjee*, Oxford University Press, Delhi, 1996, p. 182.
9. Ranabir Chakravarti, note 3, pp. 84-89.
10. H.C. Raychaudhuri, note 8, p. 598; B.N. Mukherjee, *The Character of the Maurya Empire,* J. B. Enterprises, Calcutta, 2000, pp.159-163; R. G. Basak (ed. & tr.), *Kautiliya Arthasastra Vol. II*, General Printers and Publishers, Calcutta, 1980, pp. 32-33; Ranabir Chakravarti, note 5, p. 188.
11. R.G. Basak, note 10, p. 32; R.P. Kangle (ed. & tr.), *The Kautiliya Arthashastra Part II*, Motilal Banarsidass, Delhi, 2003, p. 314; R.G. Basak, *Kautilya Arthasastra Vol. II*, General Printers and Publishers Private Ltd, Calcutta, 1980, [6. 1. 1]; cf. L. N. Rangarajan (ed., rearranged, tr., & intro.), *Kautilya: The Arthasastra*, Penguin Books, New Delhi, 1992, p.116.
12. R.P. Kangle, *The Kautiliya Arthashastra Part III*, Motilal Banarsidass, Delhi, 2003, pp.1-2 (*tasya prithivya labhapalanopayah sastramarthasastramiti*).
13. Roger Boesche, "Kautilya's *Arthasastra* on War and Diplomacy in Ancient India", in *The Journal of Military History*, 67(1), January 2003, pp.18-19, 28-29.
14. Chandrasekaran Pravin, *Kautilya: Politics, Ethics and Statecraft*, Munich Personal RePEc Archive (MPRA), MPRA Paper No. 9962, 2006, pp. 11-12.
15. V.R. Ramachandra Dikshitar, *War in Ancient India*, Motilal Banarsidass, Delhi, 1987, pp. 309-11, 316-18.
16. S.L. Roy, *Diplomacy in Ancient India from the Early Vedic Period to the End of the Sixth Century AD*, Charu Publishing Co., Calcutta (Kolkata), 1978, pp. 40-43, 69-73.
17. Patrick Olivelle, "War and Peace: Semantics of *Samdhi* and *Vigraha* in the *Arthasastra*," in Bertil Tikkanen and Albion M. Butters (eds.), *Pūrvāparaprajñā-bhinandanam East and West, Past and Present*: *Indological and Other Essays in Honour of Klaus Karttunen*, Studia Orientalia, 110, 2011, pp. 131-39.
18. R.G. Basak (ed. & tr.), note 10, p. 32; R.P. Kangle, note 11, pp. 314-15, [6. 1. 3-6].
19. R.G. Basak (ed. & tr.), note 10, p. 33, 82; R.P. Kangle, note 11, p.318, [6. 2.18].
20. R.G. Basak (ed. & tr.), note 10, p. 34; R.P. Kangle, note 11, pp. 318-19, [6. 2. 21-22].
21. R.G. Basak (ed. & tr.), note 10, p. 117; R.P. Kangle, note 11, p. 490, [13. 4. 54-55].
22. Quoted in P.V. Kane, *History of Dharmasastra*, Vol. III, Third Edition, Bhandarkar Oriental Research Institute, Poona (Pune), 1993, p. 66, fn. 93 (*nrpacakre rajake vartate svamyena cakram rastram vartayati va cakravarti*).
23. S.L. Roy, note 16, p.76.
24. J.W. Spellman, *Political Theory of Ancient India: A Study of Kingship from the Earliest Times to circa A.D. 300*, Clarendon Press, Oxford, 1964, p. 159.
25. S.L. Roy, note 16, p.76.

26. N.N. Law, "The Political Significance of the Madhyama and Udasina", in *Indian Histrical Quarterly*, 9, 1933. p. 771.
27. R.G. Basak (ed. & tr.), note 10, p. 117 (*Madhyodasinayorabhave gunatisayenari-prakritissadhayet*); R.P. Kangle, note 11, p.490, [13. 4. 56].
28. V.S. Sukthankar and S.K. Belvalkar (eds.), *The Mahabharata Asramavasikaparva*, Bhandarkar Oriental Research Institute, Poona (Pune), 1959, p. 33, [15. 11. 1] *Udasinagunanamca madhyasthanamca bharata*); N. N. Law, note 26, p. 773.
29. R.G. Basak (ed. & tr.), note 10, p. 34 (*mataptrsambandham sahajam dhanajivitahetorasritam krtrimamiti*); R.P. Kangle, note 11, p. 318, [6. 2. 20].
30. P.V. Kane, note 22, p. 216; Shri Sukhamay Bhattacharyya Shastri Saptatirtha, *Mahabharater Samaj*, Visva-Bharati Gavesana Prakashan Samiti, Santiniketan p. 400, fn. 19.
31. H.C. Raychaudhuri, note 7, p. 487, 489, 767, note 9.
32. Ranabir Chakravarti, note 3, pp. 242-243.
33. R.C. Majumdar and K.K. Dasgupta (eds.), *A Comprehensive History of India*, Vol. 3, Part I, People's Publishing House, New Delhi, 1981, p. 60.
34. B.C. Chhabra and G.S. Gai (eds.), "Udayagiri Cave Inscription of Chandragupta II", in *Corpus Inscriptionum Indicarum*, 3(11), Archaeological Survey of India, New Delhi, 1981, pp. 255-257, text-line 5 (*krtsna-prthivi-jay-artthena rajn=aiv=eha sah=agatah*); H.C. Raychaudhuri, note 7, p. 490; Ranabir Chakravarti, note 3, pp. 237-238.
35. R.G. Basak (ed. & tr.), note 10, p. 34 (*bhumyantarah prakrtyamitrah tulyabhijanassahajah*); R.P. Kangle, note 11, p. 318, [6. 2. 19].
36. R.G. Basak (ed. & tr.), note 10, p. 34 (*viruddho virodhayita va krtrimah*); R. P. Kangle, note 11, p. 318, [6. 2. 19].
37. B.C. Chhabra and G.S. Gai (eds.), "Bhitari Stone Pillar Inscription of Skandagupta," note 34, pp. 315, text-line 11 (*yudhy—amitrams—ca jitva ksitipa-carana-pithe sthapito vama-padah*), p. 316-317, cf. fn. 7; Ranabir Chakravarti, note 3, p. 239.
38. S.L. Roy, note 16, p. 94, 103.
39. P.V. Kane, note 22, p.171, 222-223; R.G. Basak (ed. & tr.), note 10, p.38 (*vijigisuh saktyapeksah sadgunyam-upayunjita*).
40. R.G. Basak (ed. & tr.), note 10, p. 34, 84; R.P. Kangle, note 11, p. 319, [6. 2. 33-34].
41. R.G. Basak (ed. & tr.), note 10, p. 78; R.P. Kangle, note 11, pp. 406-407, [9. 1. 6-7, 13-15]; U.N. Ghoshal, *A History of Indian Political Ideas*, Oxford University Press, Glasgow, 1959, p. 142.
42. Shri Sukhamay Bhattacharyya Shastri Saptatirtha, note 30, pp. 454-455, fn. 64.
43. U.N. Ghoshal, note 41, p. 139.
44. R.G. Basak (ed. & tr.), note 10, p. 35; R.P. Kangle, note 11, p. 321.
45. S.L. Roy, note 16, p. 94.
46. R.P. Kangle, note 11, p. 431, [9. 7. 72]; S.L. Roy, note 16, p. 94.
47. Shri Sukhamay Bhattacharyya Shastri Saptatirtha, note 30, p. 442, fns. 7-8.
48. Patrick Olivelle, note 17, p. 134.
49. R.G. Basak (ed. & tr.), note 10, p. 35 (*Sadgunyam-eva-etad-avasthabhedad*); R. P. Kangle, note 11, p. 321, [7. 1. 5-12]; U.N. Ghoshal, no.41, p.139; P. V. Kane, no.22, p. 223.

50. Shri Sukhamay Bhattacharyya Shastri Saptatirtha, note 30, pp.442-43, fn.10; V.S. Sukthankar and S.K. Belvalkar (eds.), note 28, p. 324, v.12. 69. 65a.
51. H.C. Raychaudhuri, note 7, p. 596; R.P. Kangle, note 11, p. 321, [7. 1. 2-4].
52. R.G. Basak (ed. & tr.), note 10, p. 35; R.P. Kangle, note 11, p. 321, [7. 1.6]; Patrick Olivelle, note 17, p. 135.
53. R.P. Kangle, note 11, p. 325, [7. 2. 1-2].
54. *Ibid.*, p. 325 (7.2); Ranabir Chakravarti, no.4, p.190.
55. P.V. Kane, note 22, p. 224; R.P. Kangle, note 11, pp. 328-331, [7. 3. 23-27, 33].
56. P.V. Kane, note 22, p. 224; R.G. Basak (ed. & tr.), note 10, p. 39, 96; R. P. Kangle, note 11, p. 329, [7. 3. 29], Ranabir Chakravarti, note 4, pp. 190-91.
57. R.G. Basak (ed. & tr.), note 10, p. 39, 97; R.P. Kangle, note 11, pp. 329-330, [7. 3. 30-31]; Ranabir Chakravarti, note 4, pp. 190-91.
58. H.C. Raychaudhuri, note 7, p. 594; Ranabir Chakravarti, note 3, p. 124.
59. R.P. Kangle, note 11, p. 330, [7. 3. 32-34].
60. D.R. Bhandarkar, "Alas Plates of Yuvaraja Govinda II; Saka-Samvat 692", in *Epigraphia Indica*, 6(18), Second Plate, Second Side, pp. 208-209, 211, text-line 25 (*kosadandatmabhumisamarpanenanate vengise*), 213; Ranabir Chakravarti, note 4, p. 158.
61. Shri Sukhamay Bhattacharyya Shastri Saptatirtha, note 30, p. 450, fn.42.
62. R.P. Kangle, note 11, pp. 338-339, [7. 6. 4-7, 13]; R.G. Basak (ed. & tr.), note 10, p.44 (for text).
63. R.P. Kangle, note 11, p. 338, [7. 6. 4-7].
64. Patrick Olivelle, note 17, p. 132.
65. R.P. Kangle, note 11, p. 347, [7.8.12-14]; R.G. Basak (ed. & tr.), note 10, p. 48 (for text).
66. U.N. Ghoshal, note 41, p. 98.
67. *Ibid*, p. 98.
68. *Ibid*, p. 99; R.G. Basak (ed. & tr.), note 10, p. 49 (*mitrahiranyabhumilabhana-muttatarettaro labhah shreyan*); R.P. Kangle, note 11, p. 349, [7. 9. 1-2].
69. U.N. Ghoshal, note 41, p. 99; R.P. Kangle, note 11, pp. 349-50, [7. 9. 16-17].
70. R.P. Kangle, note 11, p. 350, [7. 9. 33-34].
71. *Ibid.*, p. 351, [7. 9. 38].
72. R.G. Basak (ed. & tr.), note 10, p. 50 (for text); R.P. Kangle, note 11, p. 373, [7. 16. 10-12].
73. R.P. Kangle, note 11, p. 354, [7. 10. 14-16]; R.G. Basak (ed. & tr.), note 10, p. 52 (*Choraganaih-Mlecchatavibhih—pratyantassa nityamitra*).
74. R.P. Kangle, note 11, p. 354, [7. 10. 17-20]; R.G. Basak (ed. & tr.), note 10, p. 52; U.N. Ghoshal, note 41, p. 126; L.N. Rangarajan (ed., rearranged, tr., & intro.), note 11, p. 618.
75. P.V. Kane, note 22, p.18; R.G. Basak (ed. & tr.), note 10, p. 70, (VIII.2).
76. Patrick Olivelle, *Manu's Code of Law A Critical Edition and Translation of the Manava-Dharmasastra*, Oxford University Press, New Delhi, 2006, p. 205, 334, 801 (IX. 294).
77. *Ibid.*, p. 205, 802 (IX. 297 *Tesu tesu hi krtyesu tat tat angam visisyate/Yena yatsadhyate karyam tattsminchresthamucyate //*).

78. Quoted in P.V. Kane, note 22, p.18, fn. 21.
79. R.L. Mitra (ed.) and S.K. Mitra (revsd. & tr.), *The Nitisara by Kamandaki*, The Asiatic Society, Kolkata, 2008, p. 67, *Sarga* IV, v. 1 (*Parasparopakaridam saptangam rajyamucyate*).
80. M.N. Dutt (tr.) and R.K. Panda (ed.), *Yajnavalkya-Smriti*, p. 162 (I. 345 - *Arih-mitram-udasinah-anantarah-tatparah*).
81. *Ibid.*, p. 163, (I. 346 - *Upayah sama danam ca bhedo dandastathaiva ca/ samyak prayuktah siddheyuh).*
82. *Ibid.*, p. 163, I. 347.
83. Patrick Olivelle, note 76, p. 650, VII. 206.
84. *Ibid.*, p. 165, 650, VII. 208 (*Hiranya-bhumi-sampraptya parthivo na tathaidhate / Yatha mitram dhruvam*); P.V. Kane, note 22, p. 216.
85. Patrick Olivelle, note 76, p. 165, 651, VII. 212.
86. R.L. Mitra (ed.) and S.K. Mitra (revsd. & tr.), note 79, p. 152, *Sarga* VIII. v. 4-5.
87. *Ibid.*, p. 92, *Sarga* IV, v. 74 (*Aurasam krtasambaddham tatha vamsakramagatam / Raksitam vyasanebhyasca mitram jneyam caturvidham //*); P.V. Kane, note 22, p. 217.
88. R.L. Mitra (ed.) and S.K. Mitra (revsd. & tr.), note 79, pp. 182-187, *Sarga* IX, vv. 2-21.
89. Ranabir Chakravarti, note 4, p. 197.
90. R.L. Mitra (ed.) and S.K. Mitra (revsd. & tr.), note 79, pp. 187, *Sarga* IX. v. 21; P.V. Kane, note 22, p. 224.
91. R. L. Mitra (ed.) and S. K. Mitra (revsd. & tr.), note 79, pp. 337, *Sarga* XVI, verse. 32, cf. P.V. Kane, note 22, p. 171.
92. Panchanan Tarkaratna (ed.), *Agnipuranam*, Nababharat Publishers, Calcutta, 1999, p. 463, v. 1 (*prabhavotsahasaktibhyam mantrasaktih prasasyate*).
93. *Ibid.*, p. 447, ch. 233, v. 12b (*mitram janapadascaiva rajyam saptangamucyate*).
94. *Ibid.*, p. 447, verse 13 (*saptangasy tu rajyasya vighnakatrn binasayet/ mandalesu sarvesu vrddhih karyya mahiksita//*); J.L. Shastri (ed.), *Ancient Indian Tradition and Mythology Agnipurana*, Vol. 28, Pt II, Motilal Banarsidass, Delhi, 1998, p. 605, ch.233, v.13.
95. Panchanan Tarkaratna (ed.), note 92, ch.240, p.462, v. 1ff.
96. Quoted in U. N. Ghoshal, note 41, pp. 489-90.
97. Patrick Olivelle, note 17, p. 137.
98. Quoted in P.V. Kane, note 22, p. 216, fn.285.

6

Corruption in Administration: Evaluating the Kautilyan Antecedents

Tarun Kumar

Corruption is not a recent phenomenon. It has precisely been defined as a deviant human behaviour, associated with the motivation of private gain at public expense[1] and, as such, has persisted for centuries. Corruption promotes illegality, unethicality, subjectivity, inequity, injustice, waste, inefficiency and inconsistency in administrative conduct and behaviour.[2] It destroys the moral fabric of society and erodes the faith of the common man in the legitimacy of the politico-administrative set up.

There are several references to the prevalence of official corruption in ancient India.[3] But the text that provides an elaborate description of the menace is the *Arthashastra* of Kautilya. This sophisticated and detailed treatise on statecraft is essentially prescriptive or normative in nature, belonging to a genre of literature that suggests what the state ought to be and not what it really was. Nevertheless, one should realise that norms are prescribed only when digressions or abnormalities exist. This confirms the fact that corruption was rampant enough in ancient India to necessitate expert advice on how to tame it.

Kautilya[4] was a sagacious minister in the Kingdom of Chandragupta

Maurya (324/321?297 BCE). He expressed his views on a range of issues including state, war, social structures, diplomacy, ethics, and politics. He believed that "men are naturally fickle minded" and are comparable to "horses at work [who] exhibit constant change in their temper."[5] This means that honesty is not a virtue that would remain consistent lifelong and the temptation to make easy gains through corrupt means can override the trait of honesty any time. Similarly, he compared the process of generation and collection of revenue (by officials) with honey or poison on the tip of the tongue; that it becomes impossible to be tasted.[6] Based on such sweeping, albeit questionable, generalisations about the nature of human beings, he prescribed a strict vigil even over the superintendents of government departments in relation to the place, time, nature, output and *modus operandi* of work.[7] All this is perhaps indicative of widespread corruption in the Kingdom's administration at various levels.

Corruption is so obvious, and yet so mysterious. Even Kautilya reflected serious concerns about opacity in the operations of the world of the corrupt. Illegal transactions were so shrouded in mist that he compared embezzlers to fish moving under water and the virtual impossibility of detecting when exactly the fish is drinking water.[8] He also noted that while it is possible to ascertain the movements of bird flying in the sky, it is difficult to gauge the corrupt activities of government officials.[9]

During Mauryan times, superintendents were the highest officials, a position they received for possessing the desired 'individual capacity' and adequate 'ministerial qualifications'.[10] Given the general emphasis of Kautilya on observing ethics and morality in relation to the functioning of a state, it seems the selection process would have involved not just a scrutiny of the educational attainments but also the right kind of aptitude for the job including traits of honesty and impartiality. This shows that despite the greatest care taken in recruiting officials, corrupt persons made their way into the system.

Kautilya was a great administrative thinker of his times. As he argued, too much of personal interaction or union among the higher executives leads to departmental goals being compromised and leads to corruption. This is because human emotions and personal concerns act as impediments to the successful running of an administration, which is basically a rule-based impersonal affair. Similarly, dissension among executives when team effort is required results in a poor outcome.[11] Kautilya suggested that the decline in output and corruption can be curbed by promoting professionalism at work. The superintendents should execute work with the subordinate officials such as accountants, writers, coin-examiners, treasurers and military officers in a team spirit.[12] Such an effort creates a sense of belonging among members of the department who start identifying and synchronising their goals with the larger goals of the organisation, thereby contributing to the eventual success of the state.

Kautilya provides a comprehensive list of 40 kinds of embezzlement. In all these cases, the concerned functionaries such as the treasurer *(nidhayaka)*, the prescriber *(nibandhaka)*, the receiver *(pratigrahaka)*, the payer *(dayak)*, the person who caused the payment *(dapaka)* and the ministerial servants *(mantri-vaiyavrityakara)* were to be separately interrogated. In case any of these officials were to lie, their punishment was to be enhanced to the level meted out to the chief officer *(yukta)* mainly responsible for the crime. After the enquiry, a public proclamation *(prachara)* was to be made asking the common people to claim compensation in case they were aggrieved and suffered from the embezzlement.[13] Thus, Kautilya was concerned about carrying the cases of fraud to their logical conclusion.

The *Arthashastra* states that an increase in expenditure and lower revenue collection *(parihapan)* was an indication of embezzlement of funds by corrupt officials.[14] Kautilya was sensitive enough to acknowledge the waste of labour of the workforce involved in generating revenues.[15] He defined self enjoyment *(upbhoga)* by government functionaries as making use of or causing others to enjoy what belongs to the king.[16] He was perhaps alluding to the current practice of misusing government offices for selfish motives such as unduly benefitting the self, family members, friends and relatives either in monetary or non-monetary form which harms the larger public good.

Kautilya was also not unaware of corruption in the judicial administration. He prescribed the imposition of varying degrees of fines on judges trying to proceed with a trial without evidence, or unjustly maintaining silence, or threatening, defaming or abusing the complainants, arbitrarily dismissing responses provided to questions raised by the judge himself, unnecessarily delaying the trial or giving unjust punishments.[17] This shows that there were incidents of judicial pronouncements being biased, favouring one party to the detriment of others. In an atmosphere of corruption prevailing in the judicial administration as well, Kautilya perhaps wanted to ensure that the litigants are encouraged and given voice to air their legitimate grievances. He expected judges to be more receptive to the complaints and be fair in delivering justice.

Kautilya prescribed reliance on an elaborate espionage network for detecting financial misappropriation and judicial impropriety. Spies were recruited for their honesty and good conduct.[18] They were to keep a watch even over the activities of accountants and clerks for reporting cases of fabrication of accounts (*avastara*). On successful detection of embezzlement cases, Kautilya advocated hefty fines to be imposed apart from the confiscation of ill-earned hordes. If a functionary was charged and proved even of a single offence, he was made answerable for all other associated offences related to the case.[19] Since taxes paid by the people are utilised for their welfare, any loss of revenue affects the welfare of the society at large. This is precisely the reason why Kautilya explicitly argued that the fines imposed should be "in proportion to the value of work done, the number of days taken, the amount of capital spent and the amount of daily wages paid".[20]

The threat of fines being imposed and subsequent public embarrassment do deter judicial officials, to some extent, from resorting to corrupt practices. But Kautilya was proactive in laying down traps to catch public functionaries with loose morals and inclination to resort to bribery or seek undue favour. The strategy he prescribed was for secret agents to take a judge into confidence through informal channels and ask him to pronounce judgments favouring their party in return for a payment.[21] If the deal was fixed, the judge was treated as accepting the bribe and prosecuted accordingly.

Interestingly, Kautilya also dealt with the concept of whistleblowers. Any informant *(suchaka)* who provided details about financial wrongdoing was entitled an award of one-sixth of the amount in question. If the informant happened to be a government servant *(bhrtaka)*, he was to be given only one twelfth of the total amount.[22] The former's share was more because exposing corruption while being outside the system was more challenging. But in the case of *bhrtakas*, striving for a corruption free administration was considered more of a duty that was ideally expected of them.

Kautilya also warned at the same time about providing wrong information or not being able to prove the accusations. He advocated either monetary or corporal punishment for such informants so that the tool could not be misused for settling personal scores and harassing genuine officials. If an informant himself were to backtrack on the assertions he made against the accused, Kautilya suggested the death penalty for him.[23] This provision was not only draconian, but would have effectively discouraged whistleblowers. While such provisions would certainly make people think twice before levelling accusations, the threat of capital punishment was too harsh to help people root out the corrupt.

In an atmosphere of all round corruption, honesty becomes a virtue and not a desired duty. Kautilya argued for advertising the cases of increase in revenue due to the honest and dedicated efforts of the superintendents by giving rewards and promotions.[24] Bestowing public honour creates a sense of pride and boosts the motivation and morale of honest officials. They act as role models for ideal youngsters who wish to join the administration and serve the state.

Kautilya also proposed a number of measures to avoid cases of corruption arising at all. Several positions in each department were to be made temporary. Permanency for such positions was to be reserved as an award granted by the king to those who help augment revenue rather than eating up hard earned resources.[25] Kautilya also favoured the periodic transfer of government servants from one place to another.[26] This was done with the intention of not giving them enough time to pick holes in the system and manipulate it to their advantage.

Kautilya wrote that "dispensing with (the service of too many) government servants...[is] conducive to financial prosperity".[27] This is not only because of the reduction in expenditure on salary but rightsizing the bureaucracy also results in faster decision making and the transaction of government business without unnecessary delay and red tape. This effectively reduces the scope for bribery in particular and corruption in general.

It is interesting to note that the superintendents could not undertake any new initiative (except remedial measures against imminent danger) without the knowledge of the king. Kautilya, therefore, laid emphasis on some kind of an accountability mechanism. Apart from using the services of spies for unearthing cases of fraud, Kautilya also talked about an intra-departmental, self-scrutinising mechanism under the headship of chief officer *(adhikarna)* to detect and deter imminent cases of corruption.[28]

The *Arthashastra* of Kautilya thus shows that the ancient system of governance and administration was quite contemporary in operational guidelines when dealing with corruption. It also quite convincingly demonstrates that corruption is not an exclusive feature of modern times alone. The fact that the menace has survived and thrived through the ages speaks volumes about its endurance. Governments of all historical eras have recognised its illegality and devised legal instruments to tackle the problem, but they have not been able to overcome its spread as well as acceptability in society. If corruption has persisted through centuries, what is it that has stopped administrative systems from eradicating it?

Was Kautilya right in his generalisation that 'humans are fickle-minded'? The majority would disagree. Interestingly, however, even Kautilya, despite having such an understanding of human nature and behaviour, never used it to justify corruption. Rather, he realised its inevitability[29] but chose to remain positive and committed to root it out in the administration through elaborate and strict measures. This is the real significance of the *Arthashastra* as far as the issue of corruption in contemporary times is concerned.

NOTES

1. Joseph Nye, "Corruption and Political Development: A Cost-Benefit Analysis", in A.J. Heidenheimer et.al., *Political Corruption*, Transaction Books, New Brunswick, 1967, p. 967. Carl J. Friedrich gives a more qualified definition of corruption that enlarges the scope of 'private gains' by including both monetary and non-monetary benefits. See Carl J. Friedrich, "Corruption Concepts in Historical Perspective", in A.J. Heidenheimer, Michael Johnston and Victor T. Levine (eds.), *Political*

Corruption: A Handbook, Transaction Publishers, New Brunswick, 1989.

2. The listed ill-effects of corruption and its wider ramifications have been well known. See Ramesh K. Arora and Rajni Goyal, *Indian Public Administration: Institutions and Issues*, Wishwa Prakashan, New Delhi, 1996.
3. The famous Vedic prayer (*Rigveda* I, 4, 10.8) addressed to the divine power reads, "Oh Lord, knowing everybody and everything in the most accurate manner, Thou knowest the regenerate of good conduct and the degenerate, the destroyers of good works for general public. Do Thou exterminate the latter from their roots". This shows that even in Vedic times corrupt practices probably existed. Divinity was invoked to use its knowledge and power to exterminate the degenerate, the criminal and the corrupt for the sake of humanity. The reference is available at http://cbi.nic.in/coffeetable/1.pdf, (Accessed September 24, 2012).
4. Kautilya is also known as Chanakya or Vishnugupta.
5. R. Shamasastry, *Kautiliya Arthashastra*, Chaukhamba Sanskriti Pratisthan, New Delhi, 2005, p. 127.
6. *Ibid.*, p. 130.
7. *Ibid.*, p. 127.
8. *Ibid.*, p. 130.
9. *Ibid.*
10. *Ibid.*, p. 127.
11. *Ibid.*
12. *Ibid.*, p. 129.
13. *Ibid.*, pp. 123-125.
14. *Ibid.*, p. 121.
15. *Ibid.*, p. 128.
16. *Ibid.*, p. 121.
17. *Ibid.*, p. 447.
18. *Ibid.*, p. 121, 130.
19. *Ibid.*, p. 125.
20. *Ibid.*, p. 128.
21. *Ibid.*, pp. 421-22.
22. *Ibid.*, p. 126.
23. *Ibid.*
24. *Ibid.*, p. 128.
25. *Ibid.*, p. 131
26. *Ibid.*
27. *Ibid.*, p. 121.
28. *Ibid.*, p. 128.
29. The Corruption Perception Index (2011) released by Transparency International accorded New Zealand the first rank for being the least corrupt country in the world. New Zealand scored 9.5 on a scale ranging from 0 to 10. This shows that even this country is not absolutely corruption free and the scope for illegality exists in public dealings. This ranking can be accessed at http://cpi.transparency.org/cpi2011/results/ (Accessed on September 24, 2012).

7

Arthashastra Beyond *Realpolitik*: The 'Eclectic' Face of Kautilya*

Deepshikha Shahi

> *As we come to recognise the conventional and artifactual status of our forms of knowing, we realise that it is ourselves and not reality that is responsible for what we know.*
>
> —Stevan Shapin and Simon Schaffer, 1985

How responsible we have been in (re)inventing the conventional and artifactual status of the *Arthashastra*? Kautilya's *Arthashastra* has increasingly become a source of intellectual inspiration for the scholars who are particularly interested in exploring the possibilities of theorisation in Indian International Relations (IR). Their objective is not to institutionalise an Indian School of IR, but to acknowledge and appreciate the 'thinking capabilities' of the Asian world.[1] *Arthashastra*, as developed in the 4th Century BCE, is an ancient Indian script and demonstrating its contemporary relevance can serve the purpose of asserting the original thinking of the Asian epistemic communities. But how does one go about demonstrating the contemporary relevance of the *Arthashastra*? The

*This piece was first published with the same title in *Economic & Political Weekly*, Vol. XLIV, No. 41, October 11, 2014, pp. 68-74. Published with the permission of author.

academic efforts made so far have primarily relied on two methods: First, the 'application' of Kautilyan theoretical tools to diagnose the conflicts in current world politics. Second, the 'identification' of similarities in the thoughts of Kautilya and those Western thinkers who enjoy credibility in today's world.

Though the academic efforts based on these methods are significant, they are fraught with two inter-related problems. First, not many scholars who apply the *Arthashastra* have read the original work, which means that many ideas such as the Kautilyan vision of Mandala are imperfectly applied.[2] Moreover, the *Arthashastra* is frequently applied to capture the 'political', not 'economic', dimension of international conflicts. Because of its focus on power, accrued via the sharp instruments of politics, public policy analysis, and administration, the *Arthashastra* has been popularised as 'The Science of Polity' and 'Treatise on Polity'.[3] Due to the excessive stress on the 'political', the economic aspect of *Arthashastra* remains relatively under-explored in the context of world politics.[4] Second, the *Arthashastra* is mostly compared with the works of those Western scholars who are sympathetic to the notion of *realpolitik*, thereby permanently locating *Arthashastra* within the confines of Political Realism.[5] This fixation of the *Arthashastra* with Political Realism leads to an intellectual blockage. It grants the *Arthashastra* an essentially unethical, deterministic, and nativist character. Consequently, the *Arthashastra* is reduced to an intellectual instrument that is only fit to analyse the political shifts in 'balance of power' at a given time and space.

This article aims at enabling the *Arthashastra* to break free from this power-based Realist prison, thereby situating Kautilya on a broader intellectual plane that moves beyond the realpolitik. The article is divided into three sections. The first section highlights the strategic importance of reinventing the *Arthashastra*. The second section offers a critical review of the academic efforts directed towards linking the *Arthashastra* with Political Realism. Finally, the third section unfolds the 'eclecticism' inherent in Kautilya's *Arthashastra*. In order to do this, the article maps the overlap between the *Arthashastra* and a contemporary academic stream in IR—Social Constructivism[6]—that is Western in origin and transcends the constricted boundaries of Political Realism. The article concludes that 'eclecticism', or the combination of ideas from diverse range of sources, is an innovative methodology to display the contemporary relevance of the *Arthashastra*. The eclectic interpretation of *Arthashastra* not only meets the nuances present in contemporary Western IR, but also challenges the Western hegemony over the process of theorising IR.

Strategic Importance of Reinventing the *Arthashastra*: Following the Foucauldian Knowledge-Power Paradigm

Michel Foucault observes; "There is no power relation without the correlative constitution of a field of knowledge, nor any knowledge that does not presuppose and constitute at the same time power relations."[7] The Foucauldian nexus between 'forms of knowledge' and 'equations of power' suggests the importance of manufacturing knowledge for acquiring and sustaining power. As India has acquired the image of a 'rising power' in the evolving world order, the need to produce a knowledge-base to sustain this image has become paramount.[8] As the Indian strategists are guided by the overwhelming idea of India emerging as a major power and aspire to carve a space for India which would further enhance its capability to conduct political manoeuvres, the Indian scholars are increasingly viewing this ambitious turn in India's strategic thinking as a moment of opportunity for producing knowledge, which in turn would uplift the status of IR theory in India. Pratap Bhanu Mehta writes: "India has a growing footprint on the world. It will be called on to participate in shaping the world order. If it is to remain true to its own self-image, it will have to move from being a consumer of knowledge to being a producer of knowledge."[9] In a similar vein, T.V. Paul states: "As India's material power and position advance in the international system, it will be called upon to make a number of decisions both for its own interest and in the collective interests of the world. Therefore the integration of Indian IR with Global IR is urgently called for."[10] Siddharth Mallavarapu opines that such an integration process would require theoretical formulations that could explain what causal mechanisms account for political change and historical transitions.[11] Since Kautilya's *Arthashastra* deals with the shifts in balance of power as a factor of political change and historical transitions, its reinvention can help in generating the much desired knowledge-base to support the 'rising power' status of India.

In line with the Foucauldian Knowledge-Power relationship, Ashis Nandy declares that the true power of the West lies in its power to define.[12] Nandy's observation leads to the inference that the true power of India must lie in its power to define. The valid question, then, is whether Indian scholars have been able to develop a vocabulary to define the world politics. The theoretical ventures made by Indian scholars so far have been labeled as 'sub-systemic' (not systemic) theories as they essentially apply the already developed Western theoretical constructs in the regional context of South Asia.[13] S.D. Muni expresses an objection over the location of Indian IR theory within the sub-systemic category and questions in Foucauldian spirit: "Who labels theories as systemic or sub-systemic?" Though Muni rightly refutes the idea of branding Indian theoretical frameworks as sub-systemic, he does not indicate the existence of an Indian thinker whose seminal work could autonomously define world politics without using the Western IR as a referential point.[14] Since *Arthashastra* emanates from ancient Indian scholarly traditions, it most certainly qualifies as a sample of systemic theorisation. However, it needs to be adapted in accordance with the realities of contemporary modern and post-modern world before it could effectively break the myth of the inability of Indians to formulate systemic theories.[15]

An alternative way of designing systemic theories and fashioning a post-Western IR has been suggested by Navnita Chadha Behera and Siddharth Mallavarapu. Behera and Mallavarapu recommend the interrogation of the political thought of well known anti-colonial nationalists like Gandhi, Nehru, Tagore, Ambedkar, Aurobindo and Radhakrishnan while framing post-Western IR.[16] Likewise, Amitav Acharya suggests that we ought to seek theoretical insights from Nehru or Sukarno just as Western theorising has drawn from Woodrow Wilson and Henry Kissinger.[17] Though Kautilya's stature is arguably tall enough to be visualised as an Indian incarnation of Wilson or Kissinger, it is difficult to predict whether such visualisation will be acknowledged by the West. Perhaps, this problem of winning Western acknowledgement compels Kanti Bajpai to wonder if the presence of an Indian Kenneth Waltz would help redeem IR theory in India.[18] However, the transformation in the contemporary world order and India's rising status therein demands the search for an Indian knowledge-base that could match, if not overtake, the heights of Western IR.

Have Indian scholars attempted to elevate *Arthashastra* to the levels of the dominant Western IR or beyond? A good deal of academic energy has been devoted in this direction by drawing a parallel between Kautilya and the renowned Western Political Realists such as Machiavelli, Hans Morgenthau and Kenneth Waltz. Max Weber was the first to see that the writings of Machiavelli, when contrasted with the brutal realism of Kautilya's *Arthashastra*, were not as extreme as they appeared to some critics.[19] Roger Boesche compared Kautilya's *Arthashastra* with Machiavelli's *The Prince* to further explain that Machiavelli wrote a much more moderate book than he could have by omitting discussions of spies, torture, and assassins because he loved republics, trusted the people, and wanted the people to share in government—the ideas that remained foreign to Kautilya.[20] Jayantanuja Bandyopadhyaya compared Kautilya's strategy with Morgenthau's Classical Realism to assert that Morgenthau may have been influenced by Kautilya's concept of *udasina* when he speaks of the 'splendid isolation' of the balancer who waits in the middle in watchful detachment.[21] M.P. Singh observes that there is a similarity between Kautilya's writings and the Neorealist or Structural-Realist theory of IR formulated by Kenneth Waltz. He argues that Waltz postulated three levels of international politics, namely, the level where state behaviour is explained in terms of action and psychological motivations of individual functionaries of state, the level where international relations are shown to be a function of the domestic regime of state, and the level where international anarchy bereft of a sovereign power makes inter-state relations to be caused and conditioned by the structure of world politics, whether multipolar, bipolar, or unipolar. He concludes that the notions of '*saptanga* state' and '*rajamandala*' in *Arthashastra* show a similar line of evolution in international relations.[22]

Though the academic efforts towards establishing *Arthashastra* as a precursor to Political Realism have helped in evoking *Arthashastra* from its apparently dormant condition, these efforts have simultaneously exercised a delimiting impact on the scope of this incredibly vast and profound script. A critical assessment of this Realist interpretation of *Arthashastra* can create room for a broader and more useful way of reinventing *Arthashastra*.

Critical Overview of the Realist Portrayal of Kautilya: Imagining *Arthashastra* Beyond *Realpolitik*

Kautilya has been portrayed as a staunch Political Realist by a wide range of Indian and Western scholars such as Benoy Kumar Sarkar, D.D. Kosambi, Max Weber, George Modelski, Roger Boeshche, Clement A. Tisdell and Arndt Michael. Illustrating Kautilya's *Arthashastra* as a practical book of ruthless Political Realism, Sarkar states: "*Arthashastra* has to be assessed as a document of immoral practices of kings and ministers."[23] Highlighting horrendous character of the *Arthashastra*, Boesche comments:

> "Is there any other book that talks so openly about when using violence is justified? When assassinating an enemy is useful? When killing domestic opponents is wise? How one uses secret agents? When one needs to sacrifice one's own secret agent? How the king can use women and children as spies and even assassins? When a nation should violate a treaty and invade its neighbor? Kautilya—and to my knowledge only Kautilya—addresses all those questions. In what cases must a king spy on his own people? How should a king test his ministers, even his own family members, to see if they are worthy of trust? When must a king kill a prince, his own son, who is heir to the throne? How does one protect a king from poison? What precautions must a king take against assassination by one's own wife? When is it appropriate to arrest a troublemaker on suspicion alone? When is torture justified? At some point, every reader wonders: Is there not one question that Kautilya found immoral, too terrible to ask in a book? No, not one. And this is what brings a frightful chill. But this is also why Kautilya was the first great, unrelenting political realist."[24]

In his famous lecture, Politics as a Vocation, Max Weber reiterates the unethical attitude of Kautilya. He comments: "Truly radical 'Machiavellianism,' in the popular sense of that word, is classically expressed in Indian literature in the *Arthashastra* of Kautilya (written long before the birth of Christ, ostensibly in the time of Chandragupta [Maurya]): compared to it, Machiavelli's *The Prince* is harmless." The Realist readings offer a detailed account of the essentially bleak flavour of the *Arthashastra*.[25]

Underlining the 'essentialist' outlook of Kautilya's theory of *mandala/ rajamandala* (circle of states), Modelski writes: "We might call it a checkerboard model, because the basis of it is the proposition that one's neighbour's enemy is therefore one's obvious friend. This regular alteration between friends and enemies produces, for the system, a checkerboard model." Modelski adds that the 'locational determinism' implied in Kautilya's circle may need to be qualified and was, in fact, qualified in the *Arthashastra*.[26] Though Modelski discusses the possibility of 'qualifying' locational determinism in *Arthashastra*, the Realist interpretation has more often than not endorsed the checkerboard model in a geographically rigid spirit. Michael explains: "The *mandala* is based on the geopolitical assumption that the *vijigishu* (the potential conqueror state) is located at the centre of the *rajamandala*; its immediate neighbour is most probably an *ari* (enemy); the state next to the immediate neighbour is the enemy of this neighbour and likely to be *vijigishu's mitra* (friend). Behind this friendly or *mitra* state is located another unfriendly state (*ari-mitra*) and next to that a friendly state (*mitra-mitra*)."[27] According to the Realist understanding of the Kautilyan *mandala* scheme, the labeling of states as an enemy or a friend remains geographically determined. This geographical determinism leads to a simplistic conclusion that Kautilya fundamentally viewed a neighbour as an enemy and the neighbour's enemy as a friend.

Comparing the *Arthashastra* with the Greek texts and pointing out the superiority of the former, Kosambi notes, "The Greeks make excellent reading; the Indian treatise [*Arthashastra*] worked infinitely better in practice *for its own time and place*" (emphasis added).[28] Likewise, Tisdell observes:

> "In *Arthashastra*, Kautilya shows a knowledge of basic economics that had no parallels in Western economic thought until the publication of Adam Smith's *Wealth of Nations* in 1776. Although the king was at the centre of the body politic in Kautilya's time, Kautilya makes it clear that the king is bound by an implicit social contract and that the ultimate objective of the king, in economic and other affairs, should be to benefit his subjects...As pointed out here, Kautilya's conception of economics was superior to that of the Mercantilists and the Physiocrats."[29]

The claimed supremacy of Kautilya's ideas sets the stage for an academic warfare wherein the Indian scholarship is viewed in contestation with its Western counterpart, thereby tentatively narrowing down the spatial and temporal sphere of the *Arthashastra's* relevance and validity.

Though the Realist elucidation of the *Arthashastra* provides valuable insights into the Kautilyan vision of politics, it is marked with three 'hermeneutical' problems: First, the stress on Kautilya's willingness to accept 'immoralities' conveys an ethically insensitive impression of the *Arthashastra*. Second, the focus on 'locational determinism' lends a spatially and temporally rigid shape to the *Arthashastra*. Third, the emphasis on 'qualitative superiority' *vis-a-vis* the Western texts shows a 'nativist' thrust that is detrimental to the universal applicability of the *Arthashastra*. These three problems can be diluted by demonstrating the eclectic character of the *Arthashastra* that not only encompasses the features of Political Realism but also goes well with the insights of Social Constructivism.[30]

Traces of Social Constructivism in the *Arthashastra*: Unfolding the Eclectic Face of Kautilya

The core of Social Constructivism is debatably best exemplified in the writings of Alexander Wendt. Wendt's vision of international system as a product of 'social construction' goes beyond the ethically neutral, deterministic and national-interest-defined-in-terms-of-power-oriented conception of international relations developed by Realists/Neo-Realists. While the Neo-Realist theory of international relations presumes the anarchical structure of world politics and the functional similarity in states' response to anarchy, wherein states are guided by the sole motive of 'power-maximisation' in the face of 'security dilemma' flowing from anarchy understood as the 'absence of a world government', Wendt's Social Constructivism is basically a 'cultural' theory of international relations that comprises different 'cultures of anarchy' constructed by states themselves. He explains that the anarchical structure that Neo-Realists claim governs state interaction is in fact a phenomenon that is socially constructed and reproduced by states. Though Wendt endorses the anarchical nature of the international system, he problematises the Realist understanding of anarchy by arguing that the anarchy does not always imply the security dilemma originating from the absence of a world government; anarchy is what states make of it, thereby underlining the 'constructivist' capabilities of the states.[31]

In his groundbreaking *Social Theory of International Politics* (1999), Wendt draws on the philosophical views of Thomas Hobbes, John Locke and Immanuel Kant to theorise three cultures of anarchy characterised respectively by 'enmity', 'rivalry' and 'friendship'. For instance, if the system is dominated by states that see anarchy as a life or death situation (a 'Hobbesian' anarchy), then the system will be characterised by warfare; and if the system is comprised of states that see anarchy as restrictive (a 'Lockean' anarchy), then the system will more likely be based on rivalry. The three cultures of anarchy draw from three types of role structures and subject positions—enemy, rival and friend. The states have different rules of engagement, interaction logics and systemic tendencies on the basis of these three role structures and subject positions. The subject position at the core of Hobbesian culture of anarchy is 'enemy', at the core of Lockean culture of anarchy is 'rival', and at the core of Kantian culture of anarchy is 'friend', each of which involves a "distinct posture or orientation of 'self' toward the 'other' with respect to the use of violence", that is, enemies are characterised by threatening each other with violent actions in an unrestricted manner, the posturing of rivals is one of competition which includes the use of violence for maximisation of interests, nonetheless, in a limited and calculated manner, and the orientation of friends is based on alliance that prohibits violence to settle disputes and promotes collective action against security threats. Anarchy is therefore constituted by state interaction (agency), rather than accepted as a natural and immutable feature of international life (structure) as viewed by Realists such as Morgenthau and Waltz.

In contrast to Neo-Realists, and in particular Waltz, for whom anarchy is a material phenomenon from which state interests stem in the form of material capabilities and security concerns, for Wendt, the structure of anarchy consists of 'ideational' or 'cultural' elements that in turn render the 'logic of anarchy' susceptible to variation. The concepts of 'identity' and 'interests' matter a great deal in Wendt's Constructivism as they play a crucial part in interpersonal and inter-state interactions. While identities tell 'who or what actors are', interests designate 'what actors want' and illustrate their behavioural motivations. 'Interests', argues Wendt, "presuppose identities because an actor cannot know what it wants until it knows who it is, and since identities have varying degrees of cultural content so will interests." In nutshell, Wendt's Social Constructivism makes the following core claims: (i) States are the principal units of analysis for international political theory; (ii) The key structures in the states system are inter-subjective rather than material; and (iii) State identities and interests are in important part constructed by these social structures, rather than given exogenously to the system by human nature or anarchical structure as maintained by the Realists.[32]

A careful reading of the *Arthashastra* reveals a striking resemblance with Wendt's Social Constructivism. Though the Kautilyan vision of international relations, as expressed in the *Arthashastra*, revolves around the concept of 'balance of power' in the circle of states (*rajamandala*) and therefore bears a Realist inclination, it goes beyond the simplistic understanding of Realism by denying functional similarity in the behaviour of states as a reaction to the anarchical structure. The *Arthashastra* proposes an extremely complex interaction between a potential conqueror state (*vijigishu*) and its neighbouring states that can be placed under any of these wide ranging categories: (i) *ari* (the enemy); (ii) *mitra* (the *vijigishu's* ally); (iii) *arimitra* (ally of enemy); (iv) *mitramitra* (friend of ally); (v) *arimitramitra* (ally of enemy's friend); (vi) *parsnigraha* (enemy in the rear of the *vijigishu*); (vii) *akranda* (*vijigishu's* ally in the rear); (viii) *parsnigrahasara* (ally of *parsnigraha*); (ix) *akrandasara* (ally of *akranda*); (x) *madhyama* (middle king bordering both *vijigisu* and the *ari*); and (xi) *udasina* (lying outside, indifferent/neutral, more powerful than *vijigishu*, *ari* and *madhyama*). The placement of states in different categories by *vijigishu* basically implies the 'construction' of the identity of neighbouring states by *vijigishu* which is subject to change with the changing interactions between states. In Kautilya's vision, the inter-state relations have to be reassessed on a constant basis, thereby creating new opportunities of alignment in all directions.[33] The wide ranging identities of states embrace the three broad categories enumerated by Wendt, namely friend (ally), enemy (*ari*) and rival (*samantas*) that could further be identified as *aribhavin*, *mitrabhavin*, or *bhrityabhavin*.

The interests of the *vijigishu* as reflected in its policy towards different states depend on the identity-construction by the *vijigishu*. Kautilya holds that the *vijigishu* must use a six fold policy (*sadgunya*) to manage its relationship with various types of *mitras*, *aris* and *samantas* who coexist with it in a system characterised by anarchy. The formula of *sadgunya*, which sums up foreign policy, consists of six *gunas* or policies: (i) *samdhi*, making a treaty containing conditions or terms, that is, the policy of peace; (ii) *vigraha*, the policy of hostility; (iii) *asana*, the policy of remaining quiet (and not planning to march on an expedition); (iv) *yana*, marching on an expedition; (v) *samshraya*, seeking shelter with another king or in a fort; and (vi) *dvaidhibhava*, the double policy of *samdhi* with one king and *vigraha* with another at the same time. Like the differential use of violence in Wendt's three cultures of anarchy, the six policies that could be potentially pursued by a *vijigishu* towards different types of *aris*, *mitras* and *samantas* sanction the use of violence to varying degrees.

Though the policy pursued by *vijigishu* towards a particular state depends on how does the *vijigishu* 'construct' its identity, the identity of a state is not solely determined by its 'geographical location'. Kautilya writes: "Any king, whose kingdom shares a common border with that of the conqueror is an antagonist"[34] ...and "a king whose territory has a common boundary with that of an antagonist ... is an ally."[35] However, he offers specific refinements for theorising relationships with neighbouring states such as distinguishing between different kinds of enemies depending on their relative strength and weakness and allies based on the nature of one's relations.[36] The process of identity-construction is not purely material. The general rule is that when the *vijigishu* is weaker than the enemy, *samdhi* is the policy to be followed; if stronger than him, then *vigraha*. If both are equal in power, *asana* is the right policy, but if one is very strong, *yana* should be resorted to. When one is very weak, *samshraya* is necessary, while *dvaidhibhava* is the double policy of *samdhi* with one king and *vigraha* with another at the same time.[37] The assessment of the strength or weakness of a neighbouring state and then choosing an appropriate policy towards it is largely an 'ideational', not a 'material' exercise. The change in the selection of *sadgunya* in accordance with the fluctuations in the constructed identity—an ideational change—is analogous to the theory of Social Constructivism. Both Kautilya and Wendt imagined an inter-state system that could change without an underlying material change, thereby highlighting the importance of ideational change in determining inter-state interactions. Since ideational change affected the inter-state relations, Kautilya and Wendt held that the materially dissimilar states could act similarly and materially similar states could act dissimilarly, thereby breaking the notion of functional similarity and locational determinism central to the *realpolitik*.

Though Kautilya offers a variety of policy choices (*sadgunya*) to the *vijigishu*, he is not ethically apathetic in prescribing the exercise of *sadgunya*. Moral considerations do enter into Kautilya's calculations. The eclectic interpretation of the *Arthashastra* clearly demonstrates that the *vijigishu* is not only motivated by the Realist ambition of power-maximisation. It, rather, argues that the actual power enhancement of the *vijigishu* requires a moral concern for the notion of justice and tolerance that in turn depends on the constructed or imagined strength or weakness of the neighbouring state. For instance, Kautilya appeals that if a *vijigishu* has a choice of attacking a strong king who is unjust or a weak king who is just, he should actually attack the stronger king, because the stronger king's subjects, weary of injustice, will not help the strong king and might even join the war against him.[38] Kautilya further notes that if one has a choice about where to attack, it is always best to attack an unjust kingdom, because the subjects help the king who is justly behaved... Therefore, [a *vijigishu*] should march only against [an *ari*] with disaffected subjects.[39] Kautilya reminds a *vijigishu* how practical it is to be just toward his subjects because subjects, when impoverished, become greedy; when greedy they become disaffected; when disaffected they either go over to the enemy or themselves kill the master. Therefore, [a *vijigishu*] should not allow these causes of decline, greed and disaffection among the subjects to arise, or, if arisen, should immediately counter-act them.[40] Kautilya advises the *vijigishu* to win over the people in the vanquished territory and not to terrorise or exploit them for self-aggrandisement. The *vijigishu* must do what was beneficial and agreeable to his new subjects and show tolerance towards their customs, culture, mode of living, religion, deities, fairs, festivals etc. He should behave as if he was one of them, and for them.[41] Kautilya's rational preoccupation with the notion of 'justice' and his sensitivity towards the perceived needs of the 'subjects' disclose the 'eclecticism' in the *Arthashastra* that includes both a Realist concern for safeguarding selfish interests, and a Constructivist awareness of the need to mould foreign policy in accordance with the change in the perceived identities and interests of the foreign states.

Though Kautilya pays attention to moral considerations, he sanctions the unpredictable shifts in the exercise of foreign policy as a consequence of corresponding shifts in the identities and interactions, thereby belying any constancy in terms of time and space. Kautilya warns, for instance, that an ally who might do harm or who, though capable, would not help in times of trouble, should certainly be exterminated by the *vijigishu*. Likewise, if an ally with whom a king has a treaty becomes weakened, that is, if the treaty is no longer to a king's advantage, then the *vijigishu* should violate the treaty,[42] or, when after making a pact a neighbouring state intends to violate it, then the *vijigishu* should demand a gain not received or more.[43] The variety of policy options available to a *vijigishu* undoubtedly contradicts the Realist emphasis on functional similarity in the behaviour of states, thereby allowing the *vijigishu* to give diverse shapes to anarchy. Since *vijigishu* is capable of moulding anarchy in accordance with its whims, it can choose to be morally considerate, spatially and temporally unconfined, and acquire the position of a '*chakravarti*' whose authority is universally applied.

Concluding Remarks

Kautilya's *Arthashastra* is known as one of the most ancient and comprehensive Indian scholarship on the conduct of international relations. However, its contribution to the process of theorising IR is either not acknowledged by the mainstream IR scholars or if acknowledged, it is largely reduced to an exemplar of Political Realism. The dubbing of the *Arthashastra* as a Realist script grants it an amoral, essentialist and a spatially and temporally confined character. In order to enable the *Arthashastra* to surpass this Realist limit and to situate it on a comparatively broader intellectual surface, one can highlight the eclecticism inherent in the *Arthashastra* that encompasses not only the Realist line of thinking but also the Constructivist way of perceiving international relations. The diverse identities of states available in the form of a wide ranging variety of *aris*, *mitras* and *samantas*, and the broad array of policy choices or *sadgunyas* at the disposal of a *vijigishu* in the *Arthashastra*, exhibits the traces of Constructivism in the text, thereby revealing the eclectic face of Kautilya who effectively transcends the narrow landscape of *realpolitik*.

NOTES

1. Kishore Mahbubani, *Can Asians Think?*, Marshall Cavendish Editions, Singapore, 2009.
2. P.K. Gautam, "Relevance of Kautilya's Arthasastra", in *Strategic Analysis*, 37(1), 2013, pp. 21-28.
3. R.P. Kangle, A.L. Basham and G.P. Singh largely examine the *Arthashastra* as a 'science of politics', whereas D.D. Kosambi views it as the 'science of material gain'. Though Boesche breaks the compartmentalisation of the *Arthashastra* in the political and economic domains and aptly views it as a 'science of political economy', most of his energy is consumed in establishing Kautilya as the pioneer of Political Realism rather than a political-economist. See Breena Coates and Col Jeffrey Caton, "The Ultimate Pragmatist: Kautilya's Philosophy on SMART Power in National Security", in *International Society for Military Ethics*, 2010, available at http://www.veda.harekrsna.cz/library/ (Accessed on March 25, 2013)
4. Despite the economic overtone of the title the *Arthashastra*, Kautilya is barely discussed as a full blown '*arthasastri*' (economist) in International Relations. Though a number of scholars have attempted to read 'economics' in the *Arthashastra*, the lessons drawn from their readings are hardly applied to enrich the academic discipline of IR. See Charles Waldauer, William J. Zahka, and Surendra Pal, "Kautilya's *Arthashastra*: A Neglected Precursor to Classical Economics", in *Indian Economic Review*, 31(1), 1996, pp. 101-108.
5. Benoy Kumar Sarkar, "The Hindu Theory of International Relations", in *The American Political Science Review,* 13(3), 1919, pp. 400-14; "The Hindu Theory of the State", *Political Science Quarterly,* 36(1), 1921, pp. 79-90; *The Positive Background of Hindu Sociology Introduction to Hindu Positivism,* Motilal Banarsidass Publishers, New Delhi, 1985. See also Roger Boesche, "Moderate Machiavelli? Contrasting The Prince with the Arthasastra of Kautilya", in *Critical Horizons*, 3(2), 2002, pp. 253-76; "Kautilya's Arthasastra on War and Diplomacy in Ancient India", in *The Journal of Military History*, 67(1), 2003, pp. 9-37.
6. Social Constructivism encompasses a broad range of theories that aim to address questions of ontology, such as the 'structure-agency' debate, as well as questions of epistemology, such as the 'material-ideational' debate that concerns the relative role of material forces versus ideas. Depending on the relative importance attached to the roles of structure and agency, the Social Constructivism in IR can be divided into 'conventional' and 'critical' constructivism, or 'thin' and 'thick' constructivism. Common to all varieties of constructivism is an interest in the role that ideational forces play.

7. Michel Foucault, *Discipline & Punish: The Birth of the Prison*, Vintage, New York, 1995.
8. Kishore Mahbubani (2009) argues that the world is increasingly aware that we are about to enter a new historical era when Asian societies will resume the centre stage which they occupied for millennia. One reason why this is happening now is that Asian minds have re-awakened and they are asking many new questions. The biggest conceit that enveloped the minds of many Western intellectuals was the belief that as other societies modernised, they would inevitably become intellectual and moral clones of the West. Mahbubani is optimistic that this will not happen.
9. Pratap Bhanu Mehta, "Foreword", in *Muthiah Alagappa Report of the Workshop on International Studies in India*, Lee Kuan Yew School of Public Policy, Singapore, 2009.
10. T.V. Paul, "Integrating International Relations Studies in India to Global Scholarship", in *International Studies*, 43(1&2), 2009, pp. 129-45.
11. Siddharth Mallavarapu, "Development of International Relations Theory in India: Traditions, Contemporary Perspectives and Trajectories", in *International Studies*, 46 (1&2), 2009, pp. 165-83.
12. Ashis Nandy, *The Savage Freud and Other Essays on Possible and Retrievable Selves*, Oxford University Press, New Delhi, 1998.
13. Amitav Acharya and Barry Buzan label those intellectual works as 'sub-systemic' or 'exceptionalist' theorising that are situated within the Western systems of thought and seek to creatively apply them in specific local contexts. See Amitav Acharya and Barry Buzan, "Why is There No Non-Western International Relations Theory?", in *International Relations of the Asia-Pacific*, 7(3), 2007, pp. 287-312; Amitav Acharya, "Identity Without Exceptionalism: Challenges for Asian Political and International Studies", in Navnita Chadha Behera (ed.), *International Relations in South Asia: Search for an Alternative Paradigm*, Sage, New Delhi, 2008.
14. S.D. Muni and Anuradha Muni, *Regional Cooperation in South Asia*, National Publishing House, New Delhi: 1984.
15. Deepshikha Shahi, "The Indian Scholarship on International Relations and Multilateralism", in *Economic & Political Weekly*, 48(5), (2013).
16. Navnita Chadha Behera, "Re-Imagining IR in India", in *International Relations of the Asia Pacific*, 7(3), 2007, pp. 341-68. Siddharth Mallavarapu, note 11.
17. Amitav Acharya, "Identity without Exceptionalism: Challenges for Asian Political and International Studies", in Navnita Chadha Behera (ed.), *International Relations in South Asia: Search for an Alternative Paradigm*, Sage Publications, New Delhi, 2008.
18. Kanti Bajpai, "International Studies in India: Bringing Theory (Back) Home", in Kanti Bajpai and Siddharth Mallavarapu (ed.), *International Relations in India: Bringing Theory Back Home*, Orient Longman, New Delhi, 2005, pp. 17-38.
19. Max Weber, "Politik als Beruf", *Gesammelte Politische Schriften*, Drei Masten Verlag, Muenchen, 1921, pp. 396-450. Originally a speech at Munich University (1918), published in 1919 by Duncker & Humblodt, Munich. See the translated version of the full speech in H. H. Gerth and C. Wright Mills (ed. & tr.), *From Max Weber:*

Essays in Sociology, Oxford University Press, New York, 1946, pp. 77-128.

20. Roger Boesche, "Moderate Machiavelli? Contrasting the Prince with the Arthasastra of Kautilya", in *Critical Horizons*, 3(2), 2002, p. 253-76.
21. Jayantanuja Bandyopadhyaya, *A General Theory of International Relations*, Allied Publishers, New Delhi, 1993.
22. M.P. Singh, *Indian Political Thought: Themes and Thinkers,* New Delhi, Pearson, 2011.
23. Benoy Kumar Sarkar, *The Positive Background of Hindu Sociology Introduction to Hindu Positivism,* Motilal Banarsidass Publishers, New Delhi, 1985.
24. Roger Boesche, note 20.
25. Max Weber, note 19.
26. George Modelski, "Kautilya: Foreign Policy and International System in the Ancient Hindu World", in *The American Political Science Review*, 58(3), 1964, pp. 549-60.
27. Arndt Michael, *India's Foreign Policy and Regional Multilateralism*, Palgrave Macmillan, Basingstoke, Hampshire, and New York, 2013.
28. D.D. Kosambi, *The Culture and Civilisation of Ancient India,* Vikas Publishing House, New Delhi, 1994. [First published in 1964].
29. Clement A. Tisdell, *A Western Perspective on Kautilya's "Arthasastra": Does It Provide a Basis for Economic Science?*, Working Paper, 2003, available at http://ageconsearch.umn.edu/bitstream/90523/2/WP%2018.pdf (Accessed on 15 May 2013).
30. It has been argued that Realist and Constructivist ontologies are irreconcilable because Realism holds that reality is anterior to the individual, whereas Social Constructivism maintains that reality is generated by the individual. However, Gerald Cupchik (2001) challenges this irreconcilable vision and proposes the idea of 'Constructivist Realism' as an alternative ontology that accommodates Realism and Constructivism and the methods that they subtend. It is assumed that both the Realist and Constructivist approaches face the problem of selecting and analysing 'data' and are therefore subject to potential bias. While description has traditionally been viewed as preceding hypothesis testing (i.e., natural history precedes hypothesis testing), Constructive Realism perceives the two processes as complementary and in parallel. See Gerald Cupchik, "Constructivist Realism: An Ontology that Encompasses Positivist and Constructivist Approaches to the Social Sciences", in *Forum: Qualitative Social Research*, 2(1), 2001. Available at http://www.qualitative-research.net/index.php/fqs/article/view/968 [Accessed March 26, 2013].
31. Wendt calls his 'moderate' version of constructivist theory 'thin constructivism' as it 'concedes important points to materialist and individualist perspectives [of Neorealism] and endorses a scientific approach to social inquiry'. See Alexander Wendt, *Social Theory of International Politics*, Cambridge University Press, Cambridge, 1999.
32. Alexander Wendt, "Collective Identity Formation and the International State", in *American Political Science Review*, 88, 1994, pp. 384-96.
33. Arndt Michael, note 27.
34. R.P. Kangle, *The Kautiliya Arthasastra Part II,* Motilal Banarsidass, New Delhi, 1992, p. 318, [6.2.14].

35. *Ibid.*, [6.2.15].
36. Mark McClish and Patrick Olivelle (ed.), *The Arthasastra: Selections from the Classic Indian Work on Statecraft*, Hackett Publishing, Indiana, 2012.
37. P.K. Gautam, note 2.
38. R.P. Kangle, note 34, p. 354, [7.10.27].
39. *Ibid.*, p. 419, [9.4.25].
40. Harit Krishna Deb, "The Kautilya Arthasastra on Forms of Government", in *Indian Historical Quarterly*, 14, 1938, pp. 366-79.
41. M.B. Chande, *Kautilyan Arthasastra*, Atlantic Publishers, New Delhi, 1998.
42. R.P. Kangle, note 34, pp. 490-491, [13.4.54-55, 62].
43. *Ibid.*, p. 367, [7.14.7].

8

Kautilya's *Arthashastra*: The Grand Strategy

Vinay Vittal

National interests shape the policy of a state. The essential components of national interests include prestige, wealth, and security. In the *Arthashastra,* Kautilya provides an ideal framework to understand these factors that enable formulation of the national policy. Kautilya advises the political leadership to consolidate the power of the state through internal regulation of crisis and strategic control of external relations. Therefore, the *Arthashastra* is not a treatise based on general principles, but a strategy concerned with recommending practicable policies in any conceivable situation. The power lies in true interpretation of the *Arthashastra* to unravel timeless grand strategy to achieve a better peace or a continuation of an advantageous favourable situation in the future.

Kautilya's *Arthashastra* provides an insight into the ancient Indian anthology of political wisdom, theory, and the art of statecraft. It is one of the major political and strategic treatises that constitute a collection of timeless concepts. The importance and relevance of such strategies and concepts could be enriching to the contemporary world. Some of the strategies could be gainfully employed to achieve long-term benefits and resolve some of the key issues affecting numerous countries today.

Kautilya's *Arthashastra* provides guidance to a wise king to further the national interests of the state that centre on issues of security, wealth, and prestige. Throughout the *Arthashastra*, three fundamental objectives flow from one to the other: good governance (promotion of the welfare of the subjects) leads to good economy (acquisition of wealth) that, in turn, allows for the expansion of territory. The concept of diplomacy is primarily to achieve world conquest and world consolidation. Therefore, six measures of foreign policy are recommended that assist the leader in managing the state through transition from a state of decline to one of stabilisation, and from there to achieve progress or advancement. The policy to be employed depends on the relative power, strategic environment, and dynamics of the political situation. The aim of the policy is increase in power of the state at the expense of the enemy. As such, the *Arthashastra* has been identified as the first comprehensive statement of political realism. Kautilya defines war as an expression of the foreign policy of a state. He provides guidance to a king to employ the elements of national power to achieve a state of continuing advantage. Kautilya provides a *grand strategy.*

It is one thing to show that the *Arthashastra* was a valid and influential political and military guide for India more than two millennia ago, and quite another to make the case that it still holds relevance today. While there are many more recent examples of state systems that not only have attracted theorists espousing similar (if not nearly as comprehensive) political doctrines—Machiavelli's prescriptions and proscriptions in an age of independent Italian city-states, Bismarck's masterful display during the so-called Concert of Europe, or even Kissinger's perspective of the Cold War—if it can be shown that Kautilya's logic remains viable in the most modern of systems, in the most technically advanced areas, then we can truly assign it the title of *timeless classic*.

Key to Kautilya's persuasiveness is that the national policy centres *on* the population. It is *for* the people and *of* the people. The national policy provides guidance for a grand strategy that includes all elements of national power *(prakritis*): the political leadership (*svamin*), the governing body (*amatya*), the territory with people (*janapada/rashtra*), the economy (*kosha*), the infrastructure (*durga*), the military (*danda/bala*), and the allies (*mitra*).[1] The grand strategy in turn guides the military strategy.

According to Kautilya, the focus of statecraft should always be the safety and comfort of the people of the state—the word *artha* simply denotes the material well-being of the individuals. Kautilya argues that the wealth of the nation is in its territory and the people who follow a variety of specific occupations.[2] Consequently, the state has an important role in maintaining both the physical size of the state and the skills and interests of its population, and it is the highest duty of the king to provide security to the people while preserving the wealth of the people. To do so, state leadership is required to ensure maintenance of law and order and to uphold the fabric of the society. In other words, the state provides internal security and maintains social order for the people of the state.

Kautilya advises the leadership to pursue just and equitable economic policies that increase the revenues of the state, but does so in a manner that also increases the economic well-being of the population and ensures the needs of the people are met. "A king who impoverishes his own people or angers them by unjust exactions will also lose their loyalty."[3] Therefore, Kautilya advocates that the focus of the king's economic policies should always be the welfare of the people of the state. To emphasise the importance of the people, Kautilya states: "There cannot be a country without people and there is no kingdom without a country."[4] He then adds, "It is the people who constitute a kingdom; like a barren cow, a kingdom without people yields nothing."[5] In another passage, Kautilya says "a king who observes his duty of protecting the people justly, according to law goes to heaven, unlike one who does not protect his people, or inflicts unjust punishment."[6]

It is clear that a king who uses his position to further his personal wealth or satisfy earthly desires is a bad king. It should also be clear that a king who ineptly takes his country to war, expends resources and impoverishes the foundation of his power. With this logic, the duties of a king as stated by Kautilya are clear. These are protection of the people of the state from external aggression; maintenance of law and order within the state; and safeguarding the economic welfare of the people. The three objectives of the *Arthashastra* are interrelated and flow one from the other; promotion of the welfare of the subjects leads to acquisition of wealth, which, in turn, makes it possible to enlarge the territory by conquest.[7] The objectives are plain. To protect the people of the state from external threats, the military is employed by the leadership to expand the state and repel invaders. To protect it from internal threats, the police power of the state maintains order, and the just magistrates of the king fairly administer the law. Economic policies are designed to increase the wealth and welfare of the population, which, in turn, increases the state treasury. In example and in rhetoric, the king upholds the reputation and moral centre of the state. The population is ever the centre of focus. The political leadership symbolises prestige; the economy, wealth; and the military, security. Kautilya states "in the happiness of his subjects lies the king's happiness; in their welfare his welfare. He shall not consider as good only that which pleases him, but treat as beneficial to him whatever pleases his subjects."[8]

The trinity of the political leadership, the economy, and the military with direct relation to the population is a useful model that has universal application. For example, in irregular warfare, the focus of the local government, as well as the insurgents, is the population of the state, as both seek to achieve legitimacy in their eyes. The French counter-insurgency theorist, David Galula states flatly that an insurgency is a competition between the insurgent and the government for the support of the people.[9] The insurgents approach the people of the state for sanctuary, supply, and support in order to survive. If the insurgents are not able to garner the support of the population, then the chance of success is minimal. For their part, counter-insurgent operations require the judicious employment of the military to provide security and thereby acquire the support of the population to defeat the insurgency.

The financial expenditure for such operations requires the support of the population, lest the costs of security become prohibitive. Political leadership has a decisive role to play in gathering and strengthening the political will of the people to counter insurgency. The Kautilyan model would appear to hold even in modern conditions of war and insurgency. In pursuit of a counter-insurgency campaign with the stated goals of security and nation-building in countries such as Afghanistan and Iraq, the US has focused on rebuilding local economies, national military and local police forces, and legitimate political leadership with active support and involvement of the target population. Towards achieving the objective, a vital role is required by the political leadership, economy, and the military of the US, but none of this is possible without the unwavering support of the population of America. No plan for success in foreign states is possible, as Kautilya reminds us, without first attending to the needs of the population at home.

The seven constituent parts (*prakritis*)[10] of a state, as enumerated by Kautilya, provide a framework with vital significance. According to Kautilya, the power that a state can bring to bear in promoting its own interest *vis-à-vis* other states depends on how close the constituents are to the ideal. Therefore, before embarking on a military campaign, it is essential to harness the power of the different constituents of the state and, at the same time, affect the constituents of the enemy adversely. Therefore, a sound grand strategy would include the orchestration of all instruments of the national power: political, economic, military, social, informational, and diplomatic. The Kautilyan model of the constituents of a state also denotes the target structure for operations. Study of any war from this perspective highlights the significance of constituent interaction at the strategic, operational, and tactical levels. For example, during the Battle of Britain, the strong political leadership (*svamin*) of Winston Churchill, backed by a skilled Council of Ministers (*amatya*), with unwavering support of the population (*janapada/rashtra*), tapping into commercial civilian resources (*kosha*) cultivated from decades of government policy supports, assisted by an elaborate and continuously evaluated air defence infrastructure (*durga*), prosecuted by valiant military operations (*danda/bala*), supplemented by extraordinary intelligence and spy networks (use of *mitra*), all coalesced to secure victory and shatter the myth of invincibility of the German *Luftwaffe*.

Kautilya asserted that, when properly understood as a process of providing for the welfare and safety of the people, three discernible conditions of state health are evident. These are a kingdom in a state of decline, stability, or advancement.[11] When in a state of decline or in a condition of stability, each kingdom should focuses on defending itself by making alliances and solving internal problems. If the kingdom has a prosperous economy and support of the population, and is without calamities and endowed with strong leadership, it should further its national interests by advancing and conquering neighbouring states.[12]

The timelessness of Kautilya's model is readily demonstrated by the example of the state of Israel. Located contiguous to several hostile Arab nations, Israel has been involved in hostilities (*vigraha*) with its neighbours throughout its short modern history. These include open war (*prakash-yuddha*) in 1948, 1956, 1967, 1973, and 1982, with relatively unremitting clashes in the interims. Hamas, the Palestine Liberation Organisation (PLO), and a variety of state-supported terrorist organisations have waged irregular warfare (*kuta-yuddha*) against Israel without interruption. Full-scale intelligence operations, including clandestine wars (*tusnim-yuddha*),[13] sabotage, recruitment of double agents, and assassinations, have been carried out by all parties. Israel has acquired help from England, France, and the US to wage war against the Arab states (*dvaidhibhava*), has both accepted and coerced punitive treaties, has joined and rebuffed coalitions, and courted the support of former enemies. Israel has been in preparation for war (*yana*) continuously since its inception in the mid-twentieth century, but has also employed declared and *de facto* states of neutrality (*asana*) between its various wars.[14] Since 1948, from a state of relative obscurity and almost complete foreign dependency, Israel has gradually stabilised and reached a state of advancement[15] to gain a foothold amongst the Arab nations.

The dominant constituents of a State (*prakritis*) include political leadership (*svamin*), economy (*kosha*), and the military (*danda/bala*). These are pillars of a nation. They symbolise prestige, wealth and security, and represent national interests of a state. They govern the formulation of the national policy. Key to Kautilya's persuasiveness is that the national policy centres on the population. It is *for* the people and *of* the people. The national policy provides guidance for a grand strategy. A sound grand strategy would include the orchestration of all instruments of national power: political, economic, military, social, informational, and diplomatic. Before embarking on a military campaign, it is essential to harness the power of the different constituents of the state and, at the same time, affect the constituents of the enemy adversely. The grand strategy in turn guides the military strategy.

The grand strategy is recommended to assist the leader, in managing the state, through transition from a state of decline to one of stabilisation, and from there to achieve progress or advancement.

NOTES

1. R.P. Kangle, *The Kautiliya Arthashastra Part II*, Motilal Banarsidass, New Delhi, 2010, p. 314, [6.1.1].
2. *Ibid.*, p. 512, [15.1.1-2]. Explains the importance of territory for prosperity of the state to ensure welfare of the people.
3. *Ibid.*, p. 335, [7.5.27]. Describes the need for a ruler to focus on the economic policies to benefit the people of the state.
4. *Ibid.*, p. 486, [13.4.5]. Explains the importance of people of the state to the ruler.
5. *Ibid.*, p. 357, [17.11.24-25]. Describes the critical role of manpower in the state machinery.
6. *Ibid.*, p. 195, [3.1.41]. Advice to a king to ensure just rule in his kingdom.
7. L.N. Rangarajan, *Kautilya: The Arthashastra*, Penguin Books, New Delhi, 2000, p. 15.
8. R.P. Kangle, note 1, p. 47, [1.19.34]. Advice to a ruler to accord the interests of the people the highest priority.
9. Che Guevara, *Guerilla Warfare*, University of Nebraska Press, Lincoln, 1985, p. 148.
10. R.P. Kangle, note 1.
11. R.P. Kangle, note 1, p. 317, [6.2.5].
12. Roger Boesche, *The First Great Political Realist: Kautilya and His Arthasastra*, Lexington Books, Lanham, 2003, p. 4.
13. R.P. Kangle, note 1, p. 339, [7.6.17].
14. *Ibid.*, p. 321, [7.1.2].
15. *Ibid.*, p. 317, [6.2.5].

9

"*Dharmavijay* (Just War), Winning the Peace and War Without Spilling Blood"

P.K. Gautam

I. *Dharmavijay* (Just War): Liberation of Bangladesh 1971

In the language of international law and norms in war, almost all ideas and concepts are of western origin like the Latin *jus ad bellum* (the justice of resort to war) and its conduct *jus in bello* (the justice of the conduct of war). There is nothing wrong with these Western traditions, yet as witnessed in other field of international relations and law, none of the concepts seem to be based on ancient Indian traditions. The reason for this has been discussed in the past. It has been pointed out that most contemporary international law originated in Europe beginning in the 1600s and developed over the course of the last four hundred years. Most developed countries were under alien rule during the formative period of international law, and therefore played no part in shaping that law.[1] In the 21st century, more countries with ancient traditions are in the international relations and law loop, so to speak. As our knowledge grows, unearthing and revisiting ancient Indian historic traditions can augment the discourse in international laws of armed conflicts. This makes the mix richer as it includes non-western ideas.

Michael Walzer in explaining war divides the moral reality of war into two parts. War is always judged twice, first with reference to the reason states have for fighting, and second with reference to the means they adopt. This is called *jus ad bellum* (the justice of war) and *jus in bello* (the justice in war), respectively.[2] Michael Walzer has argued that the Indian invasion of East Pakistan (Bangladesh) in 1971 is a better example of humanitarian intervention. He says that "the intervention qualifies as humanitarian because it was *rescue*, strictly and narrowly defined. So circumstances sometimes make saints of us all".[3]

The former UN Secretary General Kofi Annan in a lecture in 1998 pointed out that sessions of UN General Assembly had had discussions on the international communities' possible response to threats of genocide or similar massive violation of human rights. Kofi Annan pointed out that despite the fact that the "humanitarian intervention" of India in Eastern Pakistan in 1971, Vietnam in Cambodia in 1978 and Tanzania in Uganda in 1979 had been justified, "in the eyes of the world", in all three cases the international community was divided and disturbed because of unilateralism.[4]

Recap of Events Leading to the War and its Termination

The trouble began when the Pakistani Army on March 25, 1971 disregarding the mandate of 1970 general election launched a brutal crackdown on Bengalis in East Pakistan which led to an armed struggle for self-determination. From March/April 1971 refugees started pouring in into India and a situation was reached that it was not economically possible for India to continue to host about 10 million of them. Handling refugees and facing the ire of Washington which openly supported Pakistan, India was in a very precarious position. India had deep apprehensions concerning a long-drawn guerrilla war in East Pakistan with even pro-Chinese influence at a later date if it got protracted. India negotiated the friendship treaty with the then Soviet Union in August and undertook an extensive diplomatic cum political campaign to impress upon individual countries on the realities of the situation. The regional stability also was getting worse. Thus, it was in India's national interest to get over with the problem on grounds of humanitarian intervention. Pakistan launched an attack on the Indian western sector on December 3, 1971. Based on the legitimacy of self-defence India undertook military action. Holding in the west, the Indian Armed Forces combined operations with the freedom fighters or *Mukti Bahini* in a quick and decisive way and ended the campaign in two weeks with the surrender of Pakistan's military in Bangladesh on December 16, 1971. Ceasefire in the west came into effect on December 17, 1971. The war also had the support of the people of India as there was a moral outrage and public sympathy in civil society including that of French philosopher André Malraux, and Seán MacBride of Ireland. With excellent diplomatic methods and negotiations, India overcame a number of hurdles in the politics of the UN system during all stages.

According to the official history of the 1971 war available on the web, no changes to the draft surrender document were accepted at Dacca. However, the apprehensions of Pakistani military leadership about the treatment they would get and the security of their supporters were assuaged satisfactorily. The author was a young officer near Maynamati/Comilla Cantonment in Bangladesh at that time. He recalls that immediately after the ceasefire, India gave protection to captured Pakistani troops who were easy targets for the wrath of the *Mukti Bahini*. As the author has recounted earlier in his book[5], even before ceasefire the Pakistani troops preferred to surrender to the Indian Army as they were assured of fair treatment as per the Geneva Conventions. India was party to the Geneva Conventions and Bangladesh was not as the state was not yet born as per international law. Pakistani prisoners were shifted to India as soon as possible in stages. Later, a request by Bangladesh to hand those Pakistani military officers who had committed war crimes was refused by India.

As regards the UN, after the surrender of Pakistani troops, India did not allow UN's role to be thrust upon it. India favoured direct negotiations with Pakistan and Bangladesh. The yet-to-be released official history records that some people did not want a ceasefire. They wanted India to continue dismemberment of West Pakistan. This was not accepted and in accordance with the majority of the public opinion the political spin-off from declaration of unilateral ceasefire in the western theatre immediately after liberation of Bangladesh far outweighed the military gains to be made by prolonging of the war. This move was the most effective way to demonstrate to the world that India then, as ever, was for peace and did not entertain any desire for territorial expansion.

It needs to be remembered that India never took undue advantage of over 90,000 Pakistani prisoners of war including civilians who were repatriated after the Simla Agreement of 1972. Initially, the Indian government refused to repatriate the POWs on the ground that a renewal of hostilities could not be excluded. Repatriation started late in 1973.[6] Prisoners including civilian and families were shifted in batches to their home country.

T.K. Balakrishnan has explained that the repatriation of over 90,000 Pakistani prisoners of war held in India was linked with Pakistan's recognition of Bangladesh. It was not until late 1973 that these POWs were returned. Besides, no decision about POWs could be taken without the agreement of Bangladesh. In addition of POWs, there were about 30,000 Bangladeshi's forcibly detained in Pakistan and 260,000 Pakistanis in Bangladesh. An agreement was reached in August 1973 for the repatriation of all prisoners except 195 POWs who Bangladesh wanted to try for war crimes. Pakistan recognised Bangladesh on the appeal of an Islamic Conclave in February 1974. An agreement was concluded between India, Pakistan and Bangladesh on August 9, 1974 whereby Bangladesh Government agreed to hand over 195 POWs to India, as Pakistan issued a statement condemning war crimes.[7]

A recent article on the other hand selectively shows that "Indians were clearly noncompliant with the Third Geneva Convention relating to treatment of prisoners of war. They refused to repatriate tens of thousands of Pakistani prisoners of war in timely manner, effectively holding them hostage in order to gain leverage at the peace table".[8] A secondary source from a western journal is purported to be the evidence given by the author that the repatriation took place when Pakistan brought the case before the International Court of Justice (ICJ).[9] This recent article has failed in the attempt to make India's behaviour unjust post ceasefire. In India, even now many armchair strategists in various seminars held in think-tanks argue (rather naively) that India should have used the "PW" card to get many more concessions like accepting the LOC as international boundary or even the grandiose idea to coerce Pakistan to withdraw from POK. From the conception of laws of armed conflict—the knowledge of which is today a professional requirement and is as necessary as knowledge of deployment of weapons and troops for tactical engagements—the decision of not to use the "PW card" was a just decision. Justness also gets judged later by historians. This is a fit case of just war.

Relating the Problem with Concepts in Arthasastra on Just War

In the *Kautiliya Arthashastra*[10] conquest is of three types: *dharmavijay* (just war), *lobhavijay* (war of greed) and *asuravijay* (conquest like a demon). Thus, according to *Arthashastra* liberation of Bangladesh by India should qualify as a *dharmavijay.* In other words, it was *jus ad bellum* (the justice of resort to war) and its conduct *jus in bello* (the justice of the conduct of war).

Conclusion

Concepts such as those in the *Arthashastra*[11] about conquest being of three types: *dharmavijay* (just war), *lobhavijay* (war of greed) and *asuravijay* (conquest like a demon) need to be used to support and supplement just war concepts and theories. Clearly *lobhavijay* (war of greed) and *asuravijay* (conquest like a demon) are to be shunned.

II. Winning the Peace and Wars of Armed Conflict

This is in continuation with Example I. Chapter 5 of *Arthashastra* is devoted to pacification of the conquered territory which is similar to what Michael Howard argues for. The two conditions for the use of military force to be decisive are, a) The defeated people must accept the fact of defeat and, b) the defeated people need to reconcile to their defeat by being treated as partners in international order.[12] There is also fair play in battle or *jus in bello*. It is laid down in the *Arthashastra*[13] that when attacking the enemy in open battlefield or when storming a fort, care should be taken to see that the following categories of persons are not attacked by his troops: (1) *patita*, those who have fallen down, (2) *paranmukha*, those who have turned their back on the fight, (3) *abhipanna*, those who surrender, (4) *muktakesa*, those whose hair are loose (as a mark of submission), (5) *muktasastra*, those who have abandoned their weapons, (6) *bhayavirupa*, those whose appearance is changed through fear, and (7) *ayudhyamana*, those who are taking no part in the fight. These dictums about the fair treatment of captured troops and people predates the European origins of International Humanitarian Law and the Law of Armed Conflict.

III. War With or Without Spilling Blood: Clausewitz and Kautilya

Clausewitz

Referring to or studying philosophers of war without the context needs to be avoided. For the first time, the Indian Army is embarking on the study of philosophers of war for the annual Staff College competitive examinations. This trend now will continue. Von Clausewitz's *On War* is to be studied for the examination in 2013 and Kautilya in 2014. Superficial reading of Clausewitz may do more harm. It is possible that to sound profound Clausewitzian ideas are made into mantras. What is not well-known is that this has already been debated and studied extensively in the past. The danger is that some ideas may erroneously be accepted as something new by the new breed of students without having any idea on the extensive debates on his work by European and Western scholars. This is explained below.

A powerful and negative imagery exists in scholarly imagination of Clausewitz. Appalled by the bloodshed and futile loss of lives during the First World War, Basil Liddell Hart called him the Mahdi of Mass and Violence. British military historian the late John Keegan and Israeli theorists of war Martin Van Creveld are 'anti-Clausewitzians' as well.[14] Peace research pioneer Anatol Rapoport likewise in introducing *On War* divides philosophies of war as the *political,* the *eschatological*, and the *cataclysmic.*

He places Clausewitz in the *political* category.[15] Anotol then terms the Neo-Clausewitzians as bizarre figures. He argues that "In the name of realism they perpetuate an obsolete collective state of mind which has brought humanity to the brink of disaster".[16]

No less than Major General J.F.C. Fuller, the maverick 'manoeuvre war' and 'priniciples of war' theorist, refers to volumes and pages of the English edition of *On War* to show how the understanding of Clausewitz has problems.[17] Fuller, in his study, points out that Clausewitz on page 287 scoffs at the old idea of 'war without spilling blood', calls it "a real business for Brahmins",[18] and Fuller further expands that Clausewitz considers that "to introduce into philosophies of war, a principle of moderation would be an absurdity and therefore let us not hear Generals who conquest without bloodshed."[19] Fuller's penetrating insights show that "many of his (Clausewitz's) followers were completely flummoxed and fell victims to his apotheosis of violence."[20]

Although, Fuller argued that "Clausewitz's outstanding contribution to military theory is his insistence on the relationship of war and policy", he minces no words to mention that "but of all Clausewitz's blind shots, the blindness was that he never grasped that the true aim of war is peace and not victory; therefore that peace should be the ruling idea of policy, and victory only the means toward its achievement."[21] Suffice to say that even Clausewitz's work was never completed and his ideas were accepted incorrectly as gospel truths by many scholars.

Kautilya

What does Kautilya offer on war with or without blood? His aphorism is brief. Book Ten—Concerning War deals with aspects of camps, marching, protection of troops, types/mode of fighting, morale, functions of the four arms (infantry, the cavalry, the chariot and elephants), battle arrays, and related matters. The last sutra 51 is probably the most popular idea which clearly shows mind over matter: "An arrow, discharged by an archer, may kill one person or may not kill (even one); but intellect operated by a wise man would kill even children in the womb." Surely J.F.C. Fuller and Liddell Hart would have approved of this philosophy.

NOTES

1. Keith L. Shimko, *International Relations: Perspectives, Controversies & Readings*, Wadsworth Cengage Learning International Edition, 2013, p. 223. Reference by author to Peter Malanczuk, *Akehurst's Modern Introduction to International Law*, Routledge, New York, 1997.
2. Michael Walzer, *Intervention in Just and Unjust Wars: A Moral Argument with Historical Illustrations*, Basic Books, New York, 1977, p.21.
3. *Ibid.*, p. 105.
4. As quoted by V. Kotlyar, "'Responsibility While Protecting' and the 'Arab Spring'", in *International Affairs: A Russian Journal of World Politics, Diplomacy and International Relations*, 58(6), 2012, pp. 111-124.
5. P.K. Gautam, *Operation Bangladesh*, Manas Publishers, New Delhi, 2007.
6. U.C. Jha, *International Humanitarian Law: The Laws of War*, Vij Books, New Delhi, p. 129.
7. T.K. Balakrishnan, *Foreign Policy of India: Problems and Paradoxes*, Mohini Publishers, New Delhi, 2010, p. 8.
8. Tanisha M. Fazal, "Why States No Longer Declare War", in *Security Studies,* 21(4), October-December 2012, pp. 557-593.
9. Tanisha M. Fazal, note 8. The secondary source is S.M. Burke, "The Postwar Diplomacy of the Indo-Pakistan War of 1971", in *Asian Survey* 13(11), November 1973, p. 1042.
10. R.P. Kangle, *The Kautiliya Arthasastra*, Motilal Banarsidass, New Delhi, p. 455, [12.1.10].
11. *Ibid.*, [12.1.10].
12. Michael Howard, "When are Wars Decisive?", in *Survival*, 41(1), Spring 1999, pp. 126-135.
13. R.P. Kangle, note 10, p. 490, [13.4.52].
14. See John Keegan, *A History of Warfare*, Vintage, New York, 1993; and Martin Van Creveld, *Transformation of War*, Free Press, New York, 1991.
15. Anatol Rapoport (ed. & intro.), *Carl Von Clausewitz: On War*, Penguin Classics, London, 1982, p.13.
16. *Ibid.*, p. 80.
17. Major General J.F.C. Fuller, *The Conduct of War 1798-1961: A Study of French, Industrial, and Russian Revolution on War and Its Conduct*, first published by Natraj Publishers, Dehradun in1961; First India Edition, 2003, pp.61-62. Fuller refers to volumes and pages of the English edition of *On War*, revised by Colonel F.N. Maude, and published in 1908.
18. In my reading till now this is the first time I came across Clausewitz using the word 'Brahmin'. This was obviously the influence of European Indologists who invented the idea of learned Indian pundits or professors as Brahmins. So, it is not unusual or surprising to find that Kautilya is often mentioned as Kautilya the Brahmin or the Brahim prime minister or adviser.

19. Major General J.F.C. Fuller, note 14. Reference to the use of the term 'Brahmin' in the English edition of *On War*, revised by Colonel F.N. Maude, and published in 1908 is given by Fuller in Book I, p. 287. It is clear that by 'Brahmin' it is meant intellect. Fuller like Sun Tzu is arguing that winning wars without bloodshed is the acme of skill.
20. Major General J.F.C. Fuller, *ibid.*, p. 62.
21. *Ibid.*, p. 76.

10

Kautilya's Teachings on How to "Create" Loyal Soldiers in One's Side but Sedition in the Enemy's Army

Jean Langlois-Berthelot

> *"The best soldiers are those who will not fight for money but because of their loyalty to the kingdom."*

Kautilya wrote about using money to raise an army and even of "*purchasing heroic men*."[1] One could assume he was advocating purchasing mercenaries. However, Kautilya did not believe mercenaries to be a good choice for a strong army and judged them unreliable. Indeed, mercenaries fought only for money and being dependent on this kind of soldiers could be harmful for the king's army on a long term. In fact, Kautilya had designed a classification based on a qualitative hierarchy. This hierarchy, first referenced in the Epics, consisted of the hereditary troops, mercenaries, guild levies and forest tribes. In the *Arthashastra*, Kautilya believed that the loyalty-based hierarchy of troops was a firmly embedded feature of the military system. He was able to rationalise the system.[2]

Maulas were the "hereditary" or professional troops who were connected by caste or clan with the king. These soldiers were highly considered by Kautilya because of their loyalty and fortitude. They were hereditary soldiers as the sons would adopt the family military profession and would form the equivalent of a standing army. Kautilya believed that *maulas* were the best soldiers to mobilise, especially against enemies who possessed a strong secret service. The *maulas* received certain privileges from the King. These privileges included rent-free lands and cash wages while on active service. When Kautilya stressed on the need to have enough money for the soldiers, he was merely outlining the cost of paying, supplying, and feeding soldiers. He believed that "hereditary troops are better than hired troops."[3] He described here troops made of men born in the kingdom and thus loyal to the king since birth. For Kautilya, these types of soldiers were better than strangers fighting for money. Kautilya even suggested that men of an army should know one another and that an army of friends fighting side-by-side was the most difficult to defeat.

Bhrta were those who fought for money. These mercenaries were recruited from both inside and outside the land of the king. One could wonder how these soldiers were made "near at hand and always ready to march." It could be that the king always sanctioned them some regular income which would be raised during the battle campaigns.

Srenis or *Sreni-balams* were the guild levies. These were the militias from a class of corporate guilds. The *Srenis* worked in the industry but also carried on the military profession at the same time. Even if they were a part of the royal army, they were under their own chief. They were contacted as levies and asked to join the King's army mainly in time of invasions.

These commercial-cum-military societies grew out of the need of local communities for protection of the roads and the goods from thieves. As such, they were both a source of strength and weakness to the state. They were useful in that they provided a means of local defence, including the protection of temples and shrines, and could be relied upon to provide troops during national emergency. But, they were also rather numerous and at times became powerful enough to defy the state. Kautilya, naturally, looked upon this independence with great distrust. As they were known to engage in private warfare with one another, Kautilya recommended that they be kept at odds with one another, through intrigue, so that they wouldn't become too powerful in unity.

Atavi-balam or tribals, were predatory hordes recruited from tribes generally situated in mountains or in forests. They could be useful when the King had to cross difficult terrain. They fought for pay and plunder but brought their own war apparatus. Kautilya considered them untrustworthy and undisciplined. Kautilya nonetheless lauds them as being "numerous and brave, ready to fight in broad daylight."

Making soldiers loyal to the *Raj* and their *Paltan* (Unit)

It is very interesting to see that Kautilya demonstrated the crucial importance of making soldiers faithful not only to the king and the land but also to the other soldiers—the comrades. S.L.A. Marshall's *Men Against Fire*[4] and S.A. Stouffer's *The American Soldier* (1949)[5] seem to express something very similar to what Kautilya highlights in the *Arthashastra*. Marshall's and Stouffer's books proposed a study on American soldiers' attitude in the battlefield during World War II. Stouffer showed very clearly how the combat motivation was mainly what he called the "Fighting for my buddie" motivation.

Here is a sentence from Marshall's book that strongly goes in Kautilya's sense:

> "I hold it to be of the simplest truths of war that the thing which enables an infantry soldier to keep going with his weapons is the near presence or the presumed presence of a comrade...He is sustained by his fellows primarily and by his weapons secondarily."

A research paper by Edward A. Shils and Morris Janowitz showed similar results among Germany's Wehrmacht soldiers who fought on even as Berlin fell.[6] Since these papers, the desire of "not letting your buddy down" has been the conventional wisdom as to why soldiers keep on fighting.[7] Actually, quite lately-in 2003, Marshall and Stouffer's theories have resurfaced in a report of the United States (US) Army War College: *Why They Fight: Combat Motivation in the Iraq*.[8] In India, Brigadier S.P. Sinha, author of the *History of 8 Mountain Division*, analysed something very similar during his field trip to study the 1999 Kargil operations

(Operation Vijay).[9] Very interestingly, when he asked the soldiers the question "What does a *jawan* (soldier) fight for?", the answer constantly was for the *paltan* (the unit).

King as a Role Model

According to Kautilya, King himself was responsible for national cohesion. If the people were convinced that he was following his *rajadharma*, then the kingdom would have faith in him and would fight for his cause. Solidarity between the citizens and therefore between the soldiers was based on a feeling of 'strength' and very interestingly this 'strength' has a lot to do with the perceptions on how the King behaves. Soldiers must be able to feel the power of the king as legitimate.

As Kautilya says: "Control over the senses, which is motivated by training in the sciences, should be secured by giving up lust, anger, greed, pride, arrogance and fool-hardiness.[10] The King has to follow a law inherent in the conduct of political affairs. Observe that the duty of the King, his *rajadharma*, is to live in the world as the holder of a power that exists only because it is a duty: "A king, behaving in a manner contrary to that (and hence) having no control over his senses, quickly perishes, though he be ruler right up to the four ends of the earth.[11] The King is thought by Kautilya as the holder of the power of harmony and the sustainability of his kingdom, which depends not only on his work towards the people he leads, but also with respect to itself.

Creating Fear and Distrust among the Enemies

> *"The conqueror, desirous of capturing the enemy's (fortified) town, should fill his own side with enthusiasm and fill the enemy's side with terror..."*[12]

Kautilya offers a number of techniques using fear as a prerequisite to attack a stronghold. This fear is primarily that related to the gods. It should be noted in a scathing *Arthashastra* pragmatism regarding the divinisation. It could be used for instigating fear in the enemy. It is well-reported that magical illusions were used to impress and influence the enemy.

According to Kautilya, "the soothsayers, interpreters of omens, astrologers, seers, reciters of Puranas, and secret agents, those who have helped and those who have witnessed" the power of the king in his own territory[13] must interpret all his appearances as "the proclamation of association with divinities."[14] These interpretations are mainly of two types: First, the gods deliver a message which means that the King is seen as powerful in comparison with the enemy target and the enemy would lose if it is attacked. This message is delivered to the people of his kingdom. Second, the enemy king is low and the gods want his destruction, this message is then delivered within the enemy camp by the people who have managed to infiltrate into positions that allow them to make public speeches. These people were the secret agents as inculcated by the Kautilyan techniques.

Kautilya, a good analyst of the competitions within the organs of power, advises the King to cause fragmentation, sedition, within the hierarchy of the enemy or even create it from scratch. It is then to use the fragility of the enemy hierarchy to return those who were dissatisfied against the enemy king. Kautilya goes about how, once divided, it is difficult for the enemy to rein in sedition and thereby prepare a land invasion. The agents should tell the important enemy chiefs, out of their inculcated friendship, that their king has high regard for them.[15] The king must first attract people who hold power within the system of the enemy. Seduction is the use of fear of individuals and the ability to play their perpetual quest for power. Kautilya advises to seduce ministers and generals filling their women and children with gifts,[16] by promising fortune but mostly honours and power.[17]

If the form of government of the enemy is not fundamentally unfair and if the power is left so that the insurgency is difficult breathed as the political and military elites are satisfied, then Kautilya suggests to create weaknesses in a plot to the division. Examples are described in sections 14, 15 and 16 of Chapter 1 of Book XIII of the *Arthashastra*; for example, the most significant is to decorate people by the instigation of secret agents in the opposing camp to create internal competition. Overall, the King must remain particularly attentive to any calamity (the calamities must be understood through an implicit reference to the Book VIII which defines the calamities related items, the vices of men and other pecuniary problems) to maximise profit in this crisis, usually transient, as a pivot to turn elements of enemy power against itself. In the logic conveyed by Kautilya, calamities are the best time to create discord in the camp of the enemy. If the King is considered bad and if nature (famine, disease) or Gods (in concrete appearances or legible pretended signs in nature: from the stars and wildlife mainly) seem to be turning against the enemy, if men of power in the enemy camp are looking for more power (those defined by Kautilya as having important roles in the military and political fields and non-economic) then these opportunities are to be seized. The example concludes the section by "instigating sedition" (in Kangle's translation), that is manipulation of the masses against the King in the case of a famine. But, it summarises a general mechanism for such mobilisation. "(Secret Agents) should say, 'Let us ask the king for help, if we do not get help, let us go elsewhere.' When, saying 'All right', they agree, help should be given to them by the grant of goods and grains. Thus there is this great miracle of secret instigation."[18]

Kautilya highlighted the protection of the rear and base. Of course, at the same time, he shows how attacking rears is a very valuable strategy:

> "Of the two things, slight annoyance in the rear, and considerable profit in the front, slight annoyance in the rear is more serious; for traitors, enemies, and wild tribes augment on all sides the slight annoyance which one may have in the rear. The members of one's own state may be provoked about the acquisition of considerable profit in the front. When one under the protection of another has come to such a condition (i.e., slight annoyance in the rear and considerable profit in the front), then one should endeavour so as to cause to the rear enemy the loss and impoverishment of his servants and friends; and in order to fetch the profit in the front, one should also employ the commander of the army or the heir-apparent to lead the army."[19]

A war can only really be fought against an enemy who shows itself. The infiltration of opponents' ranks allows the king to bring the enemy down. Indeed, this has two advantages: (i) the enemy is given less to react against, and (ii) from within the king can learn the weaknesses of the enemies. This allows him to open up possibilities of sowing internal dissension. This is based on a simple premise: The apparent strength of a fortress is only an illusion because from behind its wall are people who are trapped, desperate and above all afraid. Using soldiers of one's own enemy, opening an inner front, can be a very harmful tool: destruction of a structure is always easier when toppled from inside out.[20] This is the very idea present in the myth of the Trojan Horse. During the 1954-1962 French war in Algeria, the French decided to operate a very specific plan to destabilise the Algerian revolutionary forces. They built *in vivo* hundreds of 'youth camps' and 'sport training camps' under the supervision of the Center for the Algerian Youth. This center's instructors were trained in Issoire in the centre of France. The goal of these 'camps' was to educate Algerian youth with the idea of French legitimate presence in Algeria.[21]

Time and Cost

When the conqueror thinks that: "my enemy has to work with food stuffs falling short and with no comfort during the rainy, hot or cold season, giving rise to various kinds of diseases and obstructing the free exercise of his army during a shorter or longer period of time than necessary for the accomplishment of the work in hand; and I have to work during a time of quite the reverse nature", then he should make time a factor of an agreement.[22]

As emphasised by Kautilya, one of the most important factors related to time is to determine the duration of the war. Let's take an example of current war issues: The American war against Iraq cost a lot of money. This war has often been considered as a conflict that lasted a way too long. The more the war lasts the more it costs. Actually the costs of the 2003-2010 Iraq War are often contested, as academics and critics have unearthed many hidden costs not represented in official estimates. In February 2012, Brown University published a report on this burning matter called, "The Costs of War Project."[23] Seemingly, the total cost for wars in Iraq, Afghanistan, and Pakistan is at least US$3.2-4 trillion[24] (when it was said to be US$1 trillion by the American Department of Defence).

NOTES

1. R.P. Kangle, *The Kautiliya Arthasastra Part II*, Motilal Banarsidass, New Delhi, 2010, p. 406, [9.1.7].
2. S. Jeyaseela Stephen, *Literature, Caste and Society: The Masks and Veils,* Kalpaz Publications, London, 2006, pp. 210-11.
3. R.P. Kangle, note 1, p. 412, [9.2.14].
4. S.L.A. Marshall, *The Men against Fire*, University of Oklahoma Press, Norman, 1942. pp. 42-43.
5. S.A. Stouffer et al., *The American Soldier: Combat and Its Aftermath Vol. II*, Princeton University Press, Princeton, 1949, p.70.
6. E.A. Shils and M. Janowitz, "Cohesion and Disintegration in the Wehrmacht in World War II", in *Public Opinion Quarterly*, 12(2), Summer 1948, pp. 280-315.
7. R.W. Little, "Buddy Relations and Combat Performance", in Morris Janowitz (ed.), *The New Military: Changing Patterns of Organization*, Russell Sage Foundation, New York, 1964, pp.220-24.
8. L. Wong, T.A. Kolditz, R.A. Millen and T.M. Potter, *Why they Fight: Combat Motivation in the Iraq War*, Strategic Studies Institute, Carlisle, 2003, pp. 2-7.
9. P.K. Gautam, *Composition and Regimental System of the Indian Army: Continuity and Change*, IDSA, Shipra Publications, New Delhi, 2008, pp. 20-24.
10. R.P. Kangle, note 1, p. 12, [1.6.1].
11. *Ibid.*, [1.6.4].
12. *Ibid.*, p. 474, [13.1.1].
13. *Ibid.*, p. 475, [13.1.7].
14. *Ibid.*, p. 474, [13.1.3].
15. *Ibid.*, p. 475, [13.1.11].
16. *Ibid.*, p. 476, [13.1.17].
17. *Ibid.*, p. 475, [13.1.12].
18. *Ibid.*, p. 476, [13.1.20-21].
19. See Book IX Chapter III (Consideration of Revolts in the Rear), in R.P. Kangle, note 1.
20. D. Welch, *Propaganda, Power and Persuation: From World War I to Wikileaks*, I.B. Tauris, London, 2013, p. 17.
21. B. Stora, *Histoire de la Guerre d'Algerie,* La Decouverte, Paris, 2004, p. 29.
22. R. Shamasastry, *Kautiliya's Arthaśāstra*, Low Price Publication, Delhi, 2012, p. 308.
23. See www.costsofwar.org/
24. D. Baum, *Estimated Cost of Post-9/11 wars*, Brown University Updates, 2011.

11

Policy Issues Identified and Next Step(s)

I. Initial Policy Ideas in the Concept Note

Project on Indigenous Historical Knowledge

The aim of the Institute for Defence Studies and Analyses project on Indigenous Historical Knowledge is to initiate the study, internalisation, spread and consolidation of Kautilya's *Arthashastra*. The four themes for focus are foreign policy, intelligence, war and internal security as they relate to contemporary times. Issues related to what is being taught about Kautilya in the universities, location and conditions of archives and knowledge (oral and written) are also included. The material thus produced will be made available on the IDSA website as well as in sufficient hard copies, covering Kautilya's philosophy and the four themes as they relate to the contemporary times. The project would focus on:

(a) Justification for renewed focus on Kautilya in a holistic manner for contemporary times.
(b) Need for apolitical state patronage, sponsorship and finance.
(c) Providing jobs/opportunities to young university entrants so that they opt for studying Kautilya in Sanskrit, History, Philosophy and Political Science streams.

(d) Project on writing text books for the civil services institutes and military training establishments. These could also be used by the public at large. The National Book Trust could also undertake the project for the lay readers and society. The text must be apolitical.

(e) Placing the knowledge for the world as a contribution to International Studies from India.

Kautilya's *Arthashastra*

Based on this workshop and other works on Kautilya, there is a need for value addition by identifying the opportunities and gaps in knowledge which now require a new multi-disciplinary impetus of research. Kautilya's contribution to political thought and theory needs to be placed at a high pedestal using his work which encompasses disciplines of linguistics, political science and theory, military science, international relations, philosophy and history. All nations and specially countries of the subcontinent need to claim him.

More work needs to be done for that to happen. The first step is to increase the width and depth of research. There is an unending search for Asian values and security architecture. Ancient works based on the *Arthashastra* such as *Panchatantra* which is a *niti-shastra* or a text book of *niti* (the wise conduct of life) have devices of framing story best known to Europeans being that of the *Arabian Nights*.[1] The *Panchatantra* in varied forms has travelled in translation, and translations of translations; through Persia, Arabia, Syria and other civilised countries. Scholars of Persian and Arabic languages may need to do more research to find the roots in *Qalila* and *Dimnah*, Arabian Nights and even Aesop's Fables. Similarly, further research is required to find the reference to and the influence or impact of the *Arthashastra* on Persian, European, Chinese and Japanese literature and its reverse flow.

II. Policy Suggestions on Other Issues and Subjects

A. Preventing Cultural Ecocide

Sheldon Pollock, Professor of Sanskrit and Indian Studies, Columbia University, invites attention to a Sanskrit proverb: "*asakto ham griharambhe sakto ham grihabhanjane*" (It is far easier to tear down a house than to build it). Pollock terms the tearing down of the great edifice of Indian classical languages study and literary scholarship as a symptom of "cultural ecocide". There is an immense drought of knowledge and skills associated with Telugu, Bangla, classical Kannada, classical Hindi, Indo-Persian literature, *Apabhramsha*, and capacity to read non-modern scripts from Brahmi to Modi to Shikhasta where much of archival knowledge remains to be unearthed.[2]

Similarly, there is a very hazy data base on scholarship on Kharosthi and other languages that are associated with the Dunhuang archives and much of central Asia and pre-Islamic Pahlavi of Persia of the famous silk routes where civilisations and cultures flowed and mixed. On February 16, 2014, Benoy K. Behl's directed documentary 'Indian Roots of Tibetan Buddhism' was released by the Public Diplomacy Division. It is also available on the Indian Diplomacy website of Ministry of External Affairs and on YouTube.[3] In this documentary, Dalai Lama is quoted to have said, "India is our Guru (teacher) and Tibetans are their Chela (students). And we are a very reliable Chela."

Scholars point out that "Sanskrit as a living locus of epistemology, of mode of knowing and acting upon reality, has ceased to exist." What it does is only "repetition and transmission of old knowledge" like a "mere shell of a "dead" language."[4] Sanskrit needs to be revived and made popular, obviously not as a spoken language like Hindi or other usable languages but by minimum having a critical mass of Indian scholars. It is observed that people usually take up the study of Sanskrit to get permanent government jobs such as teaching in schools or colleges. The urge to study Sanskrit for scholarly pursuit is nearly absent as there appears to be no incentive. It needs to be reiterated that in order to maintain Indian cultural heritage, including an understanding of the moral content, one finds that it is vital to encourage the study of Sanskrit. We must remember that sutras are no longer passed down in the oral tradition; and since they have been committed to writing, commentaries now take the place of the living guru.

For a start, there is a need for renewed vigour on reworking on Sanskrit texts like that of Kautilya or on Buddhist Studies in a holistic manner. This needs state sponsorship and finance. It is only by providing jobs to young university entrants that it will be possible for students to study Sanskrit and then expand to the fields of History, Philosophy, Buddhist/Jain Studies and Political Science. This will also encourage school going children to opt for Sanskrit till Class XII (CBSE) for its usefulness in future in various disciplines. To begin, the study of various aspects of Indology in India by Indians should no longer be a paradox. The project will not be very costly in budgetary terms. Approximately, about Rupees 100 crores per year should be sufficient for the study of Sanskrit. Holistic centres to rediscover ancient text based on Sanskrit covering Linguistics, Philosophy, History and Political Science can be coordinated by UGC/Indian Council of Social Science Research (ICSSR).

B. Moral Issues

Another issue that will now need to be addressed is to explain the moral contents. According to Shyam Ranganathan, "Most scholars of India, though trained in contemporary university in departments of Religion, History or Indology, are ill-equipped to translate the moral content of Indian philosophy into English or other contemporary languages."[5]

C. Other Projects on Indigenous Historical Knowledge

Regional identities and histories play an important role in our understanding of India. Bhikhu Parekh eloquently explains that strong regional loyalties nurture national loyalty. "One does not need to stop being a proud Bengali or a proud Kashmiri in order to be a proud Indian."[6] And in this spirit, this beam of light on revisiting of indigenous historical knowledge must sweep and search India's proud regional traditions and histories.

The process now must gradually include revival, consolidation and familiarisation of the rich indigenous knowledge that lies buried in India. The next work may well be on South India on the *Kurals* of Thiruvalluvar. The most challenging research may be to study the various religious traditions as a study of 'phenomenology of religion' to analyse secular concepts like statecraft.[7] For example, this will demand work on revisiting secular issues from Buddhist traditions such as the philosophy of Nagarjuna and its relevance.[8] Academics would have to think of innovative means to extract and record secular literature from various periods, traditions and languages. Researchers would have to be conscious of the fact that time has come that anything with religion should not be consigned by any librarian to theology. Rich non-religious knowledge lies in Hindu, Jain and Buddhist traditions. The Gupta period is one important time for study. Eighth century CE *Nitisara* of Kamandaki, which is about 1000 years after Kautilya, is being studied to understand how the concepts and ideas were carried forward. *Kurals* of Tiruvalluvar and the literature produced by Jain scholar Somadeva Suri are a couple of texts that also need to be understood and compared.

It has been argued that "The only sacred text that we acknowledge is reason, and reason alone";[9] and that "There is no heaven, no final liberation, nor any soul in any other world... The three authors of the Vedas were buffoons, knaves and demons".[10] Kautilya's *Arthashastra* in Book II likewise under *Anvikshiki* or philosophy prescribes the study of Samkhya, Yoga and Lokayata.[11] Similarly, contrary Indian traditions such as those of *Charvakas* are also needed to be studied.

While South Indian traditions are rich and well-documented (though not well-researched and available as text books for higher education at least in other parts of India) more work needs to focus on period from 100 CE to 14th Century—a period of melting pot of Satvahana, Chera, Chola, Pandya, Chalukya, Pallava and Rashtrakuta. S.N. Prasad had rightly observed that the military history of South India remains unexplored.[12] The Chalukyas, the Pallavas, the Rashtrakutas, the Cholas and Pandyas waged wars against each other. The history of Chola, Chalukya and Pandya periods needs to be studied as it includes statecraft and issue of war, negotiations, alliances and peace. The East Indian literature/traditions need much more preliminary work.

After the ancient period, next period to be studied and analysed is the medieval period. In an occasional Paper of the IDSA written in 1999 on Sun Zi and China's Strategic Culture, M.V. Rappai listed a few Indian strategic thinkers to be studied in modern times. His recommendation now can be addressed by including the study of Kunjali Marakkar, Hyder Ali, Chhatrapati Shivaji, Sher Shah Suri, Hari Singh Nalwa and others.[13]

There are many gaps in the maritime history and traditions. The Mughal period is well recorded but awaits more translation and study. More research is required on the Sikh history and on the many *bhakti* cults which might have commented on *niti* and sociology. Regional studies such as of Shivaji, Ranjit Singh and Tipu Sultan and so on could also be developed. A lot of research has already been done on Shivaji and Ranjit Singh and one need not start from a scratch.[14] Kashmiri tradition such as Kalhana's *Rajatarangini* (The River of Kings) and *Kathasaritsagara* (11th Century) can be taken up in an integrated way with the cultural evolution of Kashmir and regions to its north. The Buddhist links to pan Himalayan areas and Central Asia can also be studied with many ancient documents now available in Kharoshthi, Brahmi, Sanskrit and other scripts and languages. More work needs to be done for the modern period by including Gandhi, Tagore and Aurobindo amongst others.

D. Chronicles of the Vanishing Oral Indian Bardic Traditions/Culture

There is a National Manuscripts Mission which seeks to record and preserve all known manuscripts in private hands. However, it is not known if there is any project that chronicles the vanishing oral bardic traditions/culture in a similar manner. This needs to be taken up by the ICSSR or any other national body under the Ministry of Culture with a similar mandate as in manuscript mission before these oral traditions are lost to us forever. Like the biodiversity loss under climate change, this tradition is vanishing very fast and barring few well-researched TV serials, plays or films, is getting distorted and commercialised.

The Centre for Armed Forces Historical Research of USI of India has begun one such project titled "The Alha Ballad Renditions of Western Uttar

Pradesh". The Alha rendition originated in about 1100 CE and is a contemporary of another famous rendition, the Prithviraj Raso. The Alha-Udal ballad was one of the most widespread oral renditions of war between the various Rajput clans of northern and central India. It was sung through vast tracts of India in all the various languages and dialects that were prevalent in this region including Bundeli, Kanauji, Bhojpuri, etc. The aim of the exercise is to document, record, analyse and publish details of this ancient but fast vanishing oral source of Indian military history.[15]

There is the *Sansi Marari* or oral folk tradition of the Punjab. *Tolkappiyam* of Sangam era in South India may also be having many military dimensions. K.K. Nair's book, *By Sweat and Sword: Trade, Diplomacy and War in Kerala through the Ages,* is a good step in this direction. The book covers *kalaripayattu* (battle training) now preserved in as a popular martial art, and *nadu-kalaris* (military academies) besides many other facets.[16] Much more work is needed to sustain this effort and bring it to the national and international level. Initially much more mapping is desired to capture the location and the state of these oral/bardic transitions all over the country.

III. State of Care and Preservation of Archives

It needs to be mentioned that palm leaf manuscripts probably had a shelf life of 300 to 700 years and scribes had to copy the text over and over again. Even today, libraries often treat a book as rare when it is thirty years old. It begins to wear out and reprints are the norm. So, there is nothing unusual in Samashastry mentioning that the manuscript might have been a century and half old.

The state of archives from secondary sources and media reports gives a poor picture. It is clear that a 'record' is both physical and logical. While the logical or virtual part is conceptual device lodged in memory and in now many translations of the *Arthashastra*, the physical part or the manuscripts are in need of a national effort for preservation.

Attitude to Archives

From policy angle, one big hurdle which needs to be addressed is our national attitude to archives. It needs to be made clear that the National Archives of India (NAI) are not the repository of any non-government text such as the *Arthashastra.* NAI holds records of the ministries and organs of the state/central government from the British period. Cultural, literary, historic and religious archives lie scattered and presumably unrecorded all over the country and probably also abroad in UK, Tibet, Nepal, Bangladesh and Pakistan. Some are still not traceable like the manuscripts on palm-leaf or paper such as fifth century *Agastya Samhita* in Daniel Smith's Catalogue of *Pancharatra Samhitas*, though printed books exist in Hindi, Bengali and Kannada press.[17]

Many historians and students of archive management have tried to bring this national problem to light such as faulty archival education and separation of archives as a practical discipline from archives as a topic of epistemological and discursive deliberations, and neglect and respect of the professional archivist.[18] The justification and arguments by some academics to show that India has a great tradition of history appear to be hollow in the light of the evidence on how we keep records of history. For the situation to improve, it is important for political leaders to show interest in the preservation of our past. The process of preservation and conservation of documents from history will be slow and long. India may lose its cultural archives and hence memories soon if policies are not quickly put in place.

Care and Preservation of Ancient Archives at Mysore

A *Times of India* news of November 19, 2011 shows that lack of funds with Oriental Research Institute (ORI) Mysore is the reason for neglect of preservation. Issues are the manuscripts peeling off, absence of locker for safe upkeep, absence of security and fireproof chambers, non-functional fumigation machine donated by Ford Foundation, etc. A cultural specialist from US consulate in Chennai had visited ORI and promised funds.[19] According to Mysore Newsletter of February 3, 2012, the US State Department handed over US$ 50,000 as grant to digitise documents and create microfilms of manuscripts.[20]

Some measures to be taken include:

(a) First step is to take stock of the manuscripts available. The second step is to create an easily accessible catalogue of ancient manuscripts including the *Arthashastra* and works of other traditions such as Jain and Buddhist secular traditions. The third step would include consideration of the issues of technology and expertise to preserve the manuscripts. Best practices and equipment for this may be required to be imported.

(b) A scheme could be initiated for the generation of funds by donations.

(c) Digitisation of all ancient archives will be needed to be done and the works to be placed in popular domain for free access including having backup storage and redundancies. Search engines need to be like that of JSTOR.

(d) It will be worth finding out if rewriting, as in the past, on palm leaf will survive or not. Is the human resource now available for such work? What will be the shape of archives in the digital age? The future of archives must now be mapped and training and education for it must be imparted.

IV. Current Status

Research and reinterpretation of the *Arthashastra* seems to be picking up. In October 2012, Tarun Kumar authored an IDSA issue brief on "Corruption in Administration: Evaluating the Kautilyan Antecedents."[21] The document was well-received as it recorded a high number of 'hits and downloads'. This was followed by other commentaries and issue briefs on the topic.[22] Another monograph was added in early 2014.[23]

Generation of Knowledge

From the domain of sanskritists, linguists and ancient historians, the concepts with fresh interpretation now need to migrate to scholars of international and security studies. The focus should remain on defence, foreign policy, intelligence and internal security. The experience of the workshop and other interactions indicates that it is possible for scholars from any discipline to use the *Arthashastra* to examine, explain or understand an on-going or future issue. Identifying what is relevant as well as the key issues is important.

Methodology

One way identified as an experiment has the following steps:

(a) Summary of a problem or issues in contemporary times.
(b) Relating 'a' with concepts in the *Arthashastra* as in the *sutras*.
(c) Re-statement of the problem at 'a' modified using vocabulary from the *Arthasastra* as established at 'b'.
(d) Reiterate strategic vocabulary so established.

One such promising workshop based on the four methodological steps as given above was held in early April 2013. A number of academics from the teaching community of IR, military officers like those who had *Arthashastra* related topic (mostly self-taught) during their dissertation in professional courses in friendly foreign countries, students pursuing master programmes or higher studies by way of M.Phil. from universities such as Jawaharlal Nehru University (JNU), Delhi University (DU), South Asian University (SAU) have shown a keen interest to learn more about the *Arthashastra*. This is the evidence of a natural demand by researchers who can complement the existing syllabus and provide alternative ideas. Four papers from the workshop are published in this volume.[24]

The IDSA has conducted a national seminar in October 2013 and another international level conference in April 2014, both sponsored by the Indian Council of Social Science Research (ICSSR). A web portal has been created in the IDSA. The web pages will be updated as and when articles get published on any period or region related to India's indigenous historical knowledge and strategic thought. Over two dozen resource persons now appear on the portal and the list will only grow.

But the most important policy suggestion is that the university system, specially those dealing with International Relations at graduate level and above, must now revise the curriculum to include the study and creation of knowledge based on the *Arthashastra* to make it relevant today with its concepts, ideas and a strategic vocabulary.

We should avoid looking for an Indian International Relations Theory in isolation from the mainstream or the so called Western International Relations knowledge body. We should rather integrate our indigenous knowledge body with the mainstream. We rather need an Indian discourse of International Relations than Indian International Relations Theory. This work and future projects are small steps towards this goal. This demands a new multi-disciplinary impetus of research. Kautilya's contribution to political thought and theory needs to be placed at a high pedestal. This is possible now by using his work which encompasses disciplines of Linguistics, Political Science and Theory, Military Science, Defence and Security, International Relations, Internal Security, Intelligence Studies, Management and Leadership to name a few. All nations and specially countries of the Asian subcontinent sharing ancient civilisational traditions need to claim him. Kautilya belongs to the world.

NOTES

1. Translator's Introduction, *Panchatantra,* Translated from Sanskrit by Arthur W. Ryder, Jaico Publishers, Mumbai, July 2011, pp.3-10.
2. Sheldon Pollock, "The Real Classical Languages Debate", *The Hindu*, November 27, 2008, at http://www.thehindu.com/todays-paper/tp-opinion/the-real-classical-languages-debate/article1383967.ece (Accessed February 12, 2014).
3. "Indian Roots of Tibetan Buddhism", video available at http://www.youtube.com/watch?v=qqkFOK7OFos&feature=youtu.be (Accessed March 28, 2014).
4. Ananya Vajpeyi, *Righteous Republic: The Political Foundation of Modern India*, Harvard University Press, Cambridge, Massachusetts and London, 2012, p. 4.
5. *Patanjali Yoga Sutra*, translated from Sanskrit with an introduction and commentary by Shyam Ranganathan, Penguin Books, New Delhi, 2008, pp. 5-6.
6. Bhikhu Parekh, "The Constitution as a Statement of Indian Identity", in Rajeev Bhargava (ed.), *Politics and Ethics of the Indian Constitution*, Oxford University Press, New Delhi, 2008, p.55.
7. One approach to study religion is of 'phenomenological epoche', an approach to the study of religion to become and to remain entirely neutral about what is studied. It requires students and scholars to suspend judgment. See Sushil Mittal and Gene Thursby, "Introduction", in Sushil Mittal and Gene Thursby (ed.), *Religion in South Asia: An Introduction*, Routledge, Oxon, 2006, pp.10-11.
8. Suggestion for studies of Buddhism in the Himalayan belt and Tibet are given in the Institute for Defence Studies and Analyses (IDSA) Task Force Report *Tibet and India's Security: Himalayan Region, Refugees and Sino-India Relations*, May 2012.
9. J.M. Macfie, "Vishnu's Incarnation as Buddha", in *Myths and Legends of India: An Introduction to the Study of Hinduism*, Rupa & Co, New Delhi, 1993, pp.183-187.

10. School of Heretics, *the Charvakas, Sarva Darshana Sangraha* of Madhava Acharya as quoted in J.M. Macfie, "Vishnu's Incarnation as Buddha", in *Myths and Legends of India: An Introduction to the Study of Hinduism*, Rupa & Co, New Delhi, 1993, p.186.
11. R.P. Kangle, p. 6, [1.2.10].
12. S.N. Prasad, "Introduction", in D.P. Chattopadhyaya (ed.), *History of Science, Philosophy and Culture in Indian Civilization*; S.N. Prasad (ed.) *Historic Perspective on Warfare in India: Some Morale and Material Determinants*, Vol. X, Part 3, Centre for Studies in Civilizations, New Delhi, 2002, pp.1-42; and J. Sundaram, "Warfare in South India—The Background", pp.167-183 and "Chola and Other Armies", pp.184-208, respectively.
13. M.V. Rappai, "Sun Zi and the Chinese Revolution", in *Sun Zi and China's Strategic Culture* (Occasional Paper), IDSA, New Delhi, September 1999, p.43.
14. The Maratha History Museum-cum-Archives of the Deccan College in Pune contains important historical records of the late 18th and early 19th centuries, useful for a student of Maratha history. There are more than 200 original manuscripts in Marathi, Sanskrit, Arabic, Persian and English in the museum collection. These manuscripts include Marathi *Bakhars*, *Pothis*, chronologies, Persian and Arabic translations of old Sanskrit works, astrological writings, diaries and poetic works.
15. The project is the initiative and brainchild of Dr. Amit Pathak (a medic) who has also carried out oral, photographic, and monumental research on the 1857 Sepoy Mutiny (War of Independence) in the Meerut Region, India.
16. K.K. Nair, *By Sweat and Sword: Trade, Diplomacy and War in Kerala through the Ages,* Centre for Armed Forces Historical Research (United Service Institution of India), Manohar Publishers, New Delhi, 2013.
17. N.B. Patil, "Agastya Samhita", in *Journal of the Ananthacharya Indological Research Institute*, Vol. IX, 2009-2010, pp. 63-65.
18. Dinyar Patel, "Our past is being moth-eaten", *The Hindu*, April 19, 2012. Sarath S. Pillai, "It's off the records", *Hindustan Times*, April 18, 2011 and "Archives and Archival Consciousness: A Postcolonial Predicament", *Economic and Political Weekly*, 47(22), June 2, 2012, pp.32-34. Shilpi Rajpal, "Experiencing the Indian Archives", *Economic and Political Weekly*, 47(16), April 21, 2012, pp.19-21.
19. H. M. Aravind and M.B. Maramkal, "'*Arthashastra*' in poor shape at Mysore library", *Times of India*, November 19, 2011, at http://articles.timesofindia.indiatimes.com/2011-11-19/mysore/30419179_1_manuscripts-oriental-library-oriental-research-institute (Accessed July 2012).
20. "ORI of Mysore University Receives Grant from US", *EDU*, February 3, 2012, at http://www.edu-leaders.com/content/ori-mysore-university-receives-grant-us (Accessed July 2012).
21. Tarun Kumar, "Corruption in Administration: Evaluating the Kautilyan Antecedents", *IDSA*, at http://idsa.in/issuebrief/CorruptioninAdministrationEvaluatingthe KautilyanAntecedentsTarunKumar121012 (Reproduced as chapter 6 in this volume).
22. P.K. Gautam, "Relevance of Kautilya's Arthasastra", in *Strategic Analysis*, 37(1), January-February 2013, pp. 21-28; "Shruti and Smriti: Some Issues in the

Re-emergence of Indian Traditional Knowledge", IDSA Issue Brief, February 12, 2013; "Understanding Kautilya's Four Upayas", IDSA Web Commentary, June 20, 2013; "Overcoming the Ways of *Matsya Nyaya*", in *Strategic Analysis*, 37(5), September-October 2013, pp. 521-525; and "The Cholas: Some Enduring Issues of Statecraft, Military Matters and International Relations", in *Journal of Defence Studies*, 7(4), October-December 2013. pp. 47-62.

23. Sachin More, *Lessons for the Contemporary Security Environment with South Asia as a Case Study*, IDSA Monograph Series, No.31, January 2014.
24. See Deepshikha Shahi, Vinay Vittal, Jean Langlois and P.K. Gautam.

Index